EVANGELIZATION TODAY

Bernard Häring

EVANGELIZATION TODAY

New edition
fully revised by the Author

Crossroad • New York

1991

The Crossroad Publishing Company
370 Lexington Avenue, New York, NY 10017

Copyright © 1990 by Bernard Häring
First published 1974. Revised edition 1990.

Printed in the United States of America

Library of Congress Cataloging-in-Publication Data

Häring, Bernhard, 1912–
    Evangelization today / Bernard Häring. —New rev. ed.
        p.   cm.
    ISBN 0-8245-1096-8 (pbk.)
    1. Evangelistic work.   2. Christian ethics—Catholic authors.
I. Title.
BV3790.H2413   1990
266'.001—dc20   91–16852
                                                            CIP

CONTENTS

PREFACE ix

PART ONE: THE VISION OF MORALS IN THE LIGHT OF EVANGELIZATION: THE FUNDAMENTAL PROBLEM 1

Evangelization of the contemporary world and appeal to justice and peace

1. The unity between the love of God and the love of our neighbour 1
2. Peace and justice 3
3. The starting point of evangelization 5
4. The signs of the times and evangelization... ... 6
   A. The objectivity of the signs of the times ... 6
   B. How can the signs of the times be discerned? 7
5. Watchfulness for the signs of the times becomes evangelization 10
6. The universality and diversity of the signs of the times 13
7. Some of the principal signs of the times 14
   A. Encouraging signs 14
   B. The challenge of alarming signs 18

PART TWO: THE MORALS OF EVANGELIZATION AND THE EVANGELIZATION OF MORALS 23

1: THE MORALITY OF EVANGELIZATON 25

1. Evangelization and the Eucharist 25
2. The Lordship of Jesus Christ 27

v

3. The irrenounceable priority in the preaching of
   the gospel   30
4. Poverty in spirit as the condition of a living faith
   and authentic evangelization...   30
5. The absolute novelty of the gospel and the novelty
   of the moral life in Christ   33
6. The evangelization confided to the ecclesial
   community   35
7. Evangelization and pre-evangelization   38

2: THE EVANGELIZATION OF MORALS   43

1. The gospel encounters an already existing morality   43
2. 'It is the decision of the Holy Spirit, and our
   decision to lay no further burden upon you beyond
   these essentials' (Acts 15 : 28)   45
3. The situation today in the light of Pauline theology   48
4. A continuous and universal task   50
5. Some models of the evangelization of morals ...   52
   A. An imperative moral system   52
   B. The evangelization of philosophies of natural
      law   53
   C. The morals of obedience and of loyalty... ...   53
   D. The morals of autoperfection   54
   E. The morals of order   55
   F. The sacramental perspective of Christian
      morals   56
   G. The morals of responsibility   56
6. The dimensions and limits of the evangelization of
   morals   57
   A. The recognition of all that is valid...   58
   B. The critical prothetic role   59
   C. The integrating role   60
   D. Openness to new dimensions and demands...   60
   E. The sacred ethos and the sanctioned ethos
7. The evangelization of canon law   61
8. A difficult transition without ruptures   68

*PART THREE: EVANGELIZATION AS RESPONSE
TO THE 'KAIROS'* 75

1: THE RESPONSE TO A CRITICAL WORLD ... 77

1. The new situation 77
2. The response 83
   A. Following Christ the Prophet 83
   B. The gospel and diplomacy should not be
      confused 84
   C. An open account of the Church's finances 84
   D. The virtue of discernment 85
   E. The necessity of teaching with discernment 86
   F. The pedagogy of faith 87
   G. Prophetic *parrhesia* (boldness) and humility 89

2: THE RESPONSE TO A DYNAMIC WORLD ... 93

1. The new situation 93
2. The response of the gospel to the dynamic world 95
   A. Re-assessment of the sense of dynamic
      movement 95
   B. The law of grace 97
   C. The power of faith and the law of faith ... 99
   D. The dynamics of the law of the Spirit ... 102
   E. The dynamics of hope 103
   F. The dynamics of natural law and of conscience 104

3: THE EVANGELIZATION OF A WORLD IN NEED
OF LIBERATION 108

1. The situation 108
2. Evangelization as a liberating response 111
   A. The Church, the sacrament of liberty and of
      liberation 111
   B. The choice of the poor 115
   C. Evangelization and political engagement ... 120
      1) The Church as the critical conscience of
         society 120
      2) The political vocation 123
      3) The various roles in the Church 124

vii

4) The pluralism of political choice 126
D. Evangelization and fighting against unjust
manipulation 128

4: EVANGELIZATION IN THE AGE OF EXODUS 132

1. The situation 132
2. The evangelizing response to this different world 133
   A. Polygamy 135
      1) The complexity of the problem 135
      2) The traditional situation 136
      3) The new approach 138
   B. Sterile marriages 146
   C. Customary marriage: the conflict between the
      uniformity of canon law and customs regarding
      the celebration of marriage 147

5: MINISTRY OF PEACE AND RECONCILIATION
   IN A LACERATED WORLD 153

1. The general picture 153
2. The response: the gospel of reconciliation ... 156
   A. The meaning of 'reconciliation' in scripture 157
   B. The Church, the sacrament of reconciliation 160
   C. The sacramentalization of the ministry of
      reconciliation 161
   D. A decisive decade of reconciliation 163
   E. Education towards reconciliation 164
      1) Education towards dialogue 164
      2) Reconciling tolerance 165
      3) A non-violent active engagement 165

CONCLUSION

A hope-filled vision of the Church of the twenty-
first century 169

Preface

The main part of this book was written sixteen years ago in view of the Synod of Bishops in the autumn of 1974. The participants of that important synod had the text available in English, Italian and Spanish. It was one of the most fruitful gatherings of bishops and other representatives of the Church committed to the convincing proclamation of the gospel to all nations. Its fruitfulness was evidenced by the beautiful Apostolic Letter of Paul VI in December 1975: *Evangelii nuntiandi*. I invite the reader of this new edition of my book to read this programmatic papal document before or after reading my book.

Having been asked to revise this book I fully realize the burning necessity of reflecting even more deeply on the role of a truly kerygmatic moral theology and pedagogy. More than ever it must be impregnated by the gospel of peace and reconciliation.

In all parts of Christianity we urge and are urged to unite ourselves in 'Evangelization of the world towards the third millennium'. We should allow ourselves a hope-filled and committed outlook towards the Church of the twenty-first century. What can we, trusting in God's grace, realistically expect? For what should we unite our energies and the renewal of our own mentality?

In the last months and years astonishing events of nonviolent liberation have happened. The main promoters realize that there now has to follow an equally generous effort of nonviolent reconciliation, of healing on all levels.

Are we ready to follow the example of the nations of Eastern Europe in a similar kind of nonviolent revolution against worldwide injustice and exploitation and even destruction of the God-given resources of creation? Does moral pedagogy bring into evangelization that dynamism of healing and liberating nonviolence that enables Christians to fulfil their role in the liberation of humankind from the oppressive and destructive systems of the arms-race and arms-trade, of nuclear threats for mutual destruction? Or are we still clinging to oppressive human traditions which contradict basic values of the gospel or at least vigilance for the signs of the times?

ix

One of the questions which underlies many other aspects is the equal role of women in evangelizing the world and the bringing of Church structures into line with the primary mission of the Church to evangelize all of humankind.

Women who read the book may kindly forgive the author if they discover pages and particular phrases where, in spite of all his good will, he did not fully succeed in using an inclusive language. They may take into account that I did not aim at this when challenging the age-old paternalism, although I am fully aware of the task that both, man and woman, have of liberating culture and Church institutions from paternalistic neurosis. This, too, is a matter of mutual healing.

PART ONE

THE VISION OF MORALS IN THE LIGHT OF EVANGELIZATION: THE FUNDAMENTAL PROBLEM

Only if we see clearly in what sense the moral message of the Church and the moral life of the faithful are, in God's plan, integral parts of witnessing to the faith and of evangelization in today's world, will the fruitfulness of such a perspective in relation to a realistic approach to the more burning questions of morals today be revealed.

The term 'evangelization' is understood in the larger sense of testimony and proclamation of the mystery of salvation, not only as propagation of the faith, but also as its perennial deepening and vitalization. However, I give particular attention to the evangelization of culture and of men who do not yet or no longer call themselves Christians, and of new generations which feel the necessity of new forms of evangelization.[1]

EVANGELIZATION OF THE CONTEMPORARY WORLD AND APPEAL TO JUSTICE AND PEACE

It seems providential that the Holy Father should have chosen *Evangelization of the world today* as the theme for the coming synod of bishops*, and that equally fundamental one of *Reconciliation* for the Holy Year of 1975. These two great themes are united in a biblical vision, thus indicating to us the way to arrive at a moral message typically Christian for the world today.

1. *The unity between the love of God and the love of our neighbour*

The characteristic note of Christian moral theology is the perfect synthesis between love of God and love of neighbour, between cult and its truthfulness through a life which honours God the Father, between knowledge of God and knowledge

---

*The reader is reminded that this book was originally published in 1974 in view of the Synod in that year.

1

of man, between eschatological hope and zeal for the present world. God reveals himself as Love by manifesting his love for man. Man on his part can reach existential knowledge of God who is Love only in so far as he is united to God in his love for all men. For a Christian, a cult which does not bear fruit in love of one's neighbour and in justice directed towards the life of the world, is worth nothing. For a Christian the eschatological hope is worth nothing when it is not manifested in watchfulness for present opportunities and in a commitment to the good and salvation of man.

Paul Claudel's statement has already become famous: 'Certainly we love Christ, but nothing in the world will make us love morals' (in the sense of moralism!); and Charles Pèguy has affirmed it in a way still more stinging: 'Moralism inhibits the penetration of the Spirit.' Today we find ourselves in great danger of reducing our obligation towards the world to a new type of moralism, that of an appeal to be involved or of a threat; on the other hand, the man of today rightly refuses a message of salvation which does not show itself to be effective and does not manifestly press for the solidarity of the human race and the promotion of each person. Moral theology must think over its structures and norms in the light of evangelization. If it is truly to become gospel, it must reflect the good news of God who is Love and who gives us the capacity to love each other in an authentically redeemed manner. A dogmatic that is chiefly characterized by an objectivism closed to the dynamics of life is no longer possible; neither can we speak any longer of obligations and sins without understanding that, at least implicitly, we are always speaking of God.

No longer acceptable either is a dogmatic or morals whose authority derives merely or mainly from obedience to the established order, that is, to ecclesiastical authority. If, on the contrary, the Church proclaims the good news of God who is Love dynamically, directing it towards the growth of man, towards justice and peace, the moral appeal thereby becomes profoundly motivated and attractive.

The political theology of recent years has studied the interdependence between religious expression and life in the secular city. Man is always influenced by life in the secular city, which makes him form for himself a religious expression similar to that of the prevailing social order. However, every religious position, every doctrine, every method of teaching used, every imperative proclaimed will inevitably influence the life of the earthly city. This influence can become negative when in the life of the Church and of each man there is a lack of full awareness, of how religious expression echoes in the earthly city, in the human life.[2]

2. *Peace and justice*

The total messianic hope and the complete revelation in Jesus Christ can be synthesized in the words *shalom* (peace) and *dikaiosyne* (justice, that is, new justice and reconciliation).[3] Here we are truly in the centre of the good news.

It is necessary to see the religious as well as the moral aspect of these fundamental biblical concepts. If in fact we follow the vision of scripture there is no more possibility of a disincarnated supranaturalism than there is of an intramundane messianism. *Shalom* can be received and recognized for what it is — the free gift of God — only in faith, that is, in the humble prayer of supplication and thanksgiving. But it is important to note that peace, *shalom*, is not closed up in one single prospect: it is peace at all levels. In the first place, it is peace with God; God communicates his peace to us through Jesus Christ in the Holy Spirit as gift. And this gift cannot be received by us without becoming messenger and instrument on all levels: in the family, in society, in the Church, in national and international life.[4] Peace is not something that is static; it finds us in a world loaded with tensions and full of sin. Peace therefore communicates itself as reconciliation: to accept it with gratitude means to become ambassadors of it. God, who in Christ has reconciled us to himself, has confided to the entire Church, and in a particular way to the apostles and their successors, the ministry of reconciliation. 'That is, God was in Christ reconciling the world to himself, not counting their trespasses against them, and entrusting to us the message of reconciliation' (2 Cor 5: 19ff). The fact that Christ is the reconciler becomes for every man and for every human community grace, and an appeal: reconcile yourselves with God and between yourselves.

A central concept of Pauline moral theology is that of *dikaiosyne* (righteousness), justification. In a mysterious solidarity Jesus Christ willed to carry the burden of our sins and has justified us by pure grace. This is an invitation to all to become in him the justice of God (2 Cor 5 : 21). Like the concept of *shalom*, so also that of justification expresses in the first place the gratuity of the gift of God, and it is precisely this gratuity which, united to the totality of the gift, becomes the most urgent appeal; it transforms the faithful into instruments of justice on all levels. It is a matter of the 'new justice' thus certainly not that of businessmen (commutative justice) nor that of the Pharisees ('according to the law'). Justification in Jesus Christ is the expression of God's family, in which each one carries the burden of his brother; Christ, in the new justice, wanted to receive baptism (cf. Mt 3 : 15) so that all of us might be baptized in one Spirit and bear fruit in unity and solidarity, in justice and love.

These biblical concepts — *shalom*, justice, reconciliation — do not allow a disincarnate verticalism nor a horizontalism closed to supernatural perspectives. The gift of peace, of the new justice and of reconciliation is an eschatological reality, brought however by the Word Incarnate: one cannot confide in eschatology without a continuous effort to incarnate this promise and this hope in the whole reality of the world in which we live. The greater the intensity with which man as an individual and the human community receive the message of peace, of justice and of reconciliation, the more they will radically accept also the mission to become effective signs and witnesses of it, without permitting themselves to forget any one of the human dimensions. Hope in the absolute future is possible only in courageous commitment to the immediate future. This zeal is stimulated by thanksgiving for all God has done for us and given to us since the beginning of creation, in the incarnation, passion, death, resurrection and ascension of Christ and in the mission of the Spirit. The memorial of the paschal mysteries, till the return of Christ, in thanksgiving and in hope, brings about watchfulness for the present moment and sustains our readiness to use fully the present opportunities (cf. Eph 5 : 16).

It is not possible to celebrate fruitfully the Eucharist or any other sacrament, nor is it possible to receive the gospel of reconciliation in Jesus Christ, when the ecclesial community and the person are cut off from, or alien to, historical reality. Evangelization as well as the celebration of the mysteries of God is an event in the history of salvation; it is a grace and a call to engage in this history as co-creators, co-operators with God, and co-revealers of his justice and love.

3. *The starting point of evangelization*

The starting point of everything in an absolute sense is always God, the Love which efficaciously reveals itself as salvation, justice and reconciliation for men. In another sense, perhaps not less concrete, the starting point is the human experience: divine revelation is never separated from the total experience of man. We cannot separate the full consciousness of Christ as being the beloved Son sent by the Father from the human experience which he had of himself and of the world around him. Every form and pattern of the knowledge of God, especially those expressed in words, are, up to a certain point, conditioned by human experiences.

In view of the centrality of the mystery of the Word Incarnate, it is necessary to stress this second point of departure, above all in evangelization. We cannot speak to people of today without knowing them, without uniting ourselves existentially to their experiences, joys, hopes and sufferings. Jesus the Incarnate Word has always spoken in parables. In the parable the first place is given to the concrete experience known by those who listen to it. But the Lord does not remain closed in the narrow limits of this experience; this experience is only a starting point for much wider and higher horizons.[5]

Christ is the Prophet;[6] in him we find the perfect synthesis of zeal for the glory of God and compassion for man, of zeal for justice and peace, and for that justice which makes us similar to God who is infinitely merciful (cf. Lk 6 : 36). In every valid and true experience of hunger and thirst for justice, of oblative and passionate love, of desire for peace and reconciliation there is already inherent a presence of Christ who thus prepares the full message and reality.

4. *The signs of the times and evangelization*

To be able to formulate and communicate the message of salvation which remains always identical, it is necessary to know human experience in its favourable aspects and also in its dangerous ones. Above all, it is necessary to know well the situation of the people and the community to which we are sent as messengers of salvation. It is not a question of knowing every detail, fact or statistic, nor of knowing every aspect of events or of science; it is a question of scrutinizing and discerning those events, processes and interdependences which have profound repercussions on the whole moral, religious and social life, in fact on life in all its manifestations.

A. *The objectivity of the signs of the times*[7]

We can speak of *vox temporum, vox Dei* (God calling us through the signs of the times) only because God is the Lord of heaven and earth, because the Creator and Redeemer is present in the whole of human history and thus the signs of his presence are impressed in history. Some of these signs of the times are more perceptible in the Church, others are perhaps more evident in the secular world: but it is a matter of only one order of creation and salvation, and thus it is unthinkable that there should be no profound interdependence between the history of the Church and the total history of man. It will be enough to reflect on how the experience of the solidarity of mankind in the world today has stimulated and fostered ecumenism. The principal events which influence the existence of man are a *locus theologicus* which neither scientific theology nor evangelization can relinquish. God has not shut himself up in a book nor in a situation. The same God who revealed his most active presence in the incarnation, passion, death and resurrection is present in the whole of history: the Spirit of God renews the face of the earth and the hearts of men.[8]

But we must not speak of the signs of the times as a *locus theologicus* to be put side by side with the revelation in Jesus Christ: he is the ultimate and definitive Word of the Father to the world, but he is also the Word in which everything has been created. The whole creation, and therefore the whole of history, has the character of a word-event, of an event-revealer. And therefore, since everything has its centre in the Word Incarnate, particularly in the paschal mystery and in the eschatological hope, the signs of the times do not stand beside the revelation in Jesus Christ but are fully integrated in its light: they are part of the full revelation in him who is the Word of the Father. Consequently, the signs of the times can never contradict the revelation which is received in the Son and which constitutes the deposit of faith.

B. *How can the signs of the times be discerned?*[9]

1. I have already stressed that we can speak of the signs of the times, and discern them as the presence of God, only *in the light of faith in Jesus Christ.* Only to those who believe in creation through the Word, in the coming of Christ and in the final hope of man, can the events of history disclose themselves as signs of the presence of God, that is, as signs of the times.

2. He who says faith says also, necessarily, *community of faith and salvation.* God does not let himself be monopolized by an individual person or group: he reveals himself always as Lord and Father of all people. Christ wants the faith to be preached, lived and witnessed to in the community of salvation, the community of his disciples. The Spirit sent to us by Christ operates in all, by means of all and for all. The individualist, even if he cares for his own salvation, can never be in a position to discern the signs of the times. To know in the greatest measure possible the plan of God for our time, we must unite ourselves in faith, in a search, in meditation and in prayer. And since God operates in all creation and in the entire history of man, it is necessary that the disciples of Christ unite themselves to all others, with sincere consciences in the search for the true and the good, in discerning and making full use of the signs of the times, pursuing and encouraging just solutions to the many problems which continually arise in economic, cultural, political and social life and so on . . . (cf. *Gaudium et spes,* 16).

3. The signs of the times are considered signs of the presence of God, Creator and Saviour: it is therefore evident that man

7

cannot discern them without *the grace of the Holy Spirit.* To be vigilant, and to know how to discern, demands personal prayer and community prayer. In this regard, it must be said that it is certainly not sufficient to recite prayers. It is necessary that there be that life of prayer which gives liberty to the Spirit who cries out in us: 'Abba! Father!' And this prayer becomes spontaneity, creativity, openness, sign of the presence of the Spirit. Only a community of persons engaged in personal and community prayer which is conscious of the presence of God, who calls and gathers all men together, will be capable of listening to the voice of the times and understanding the more urgent signs of the presence of God in human history.[10]

4. Confidence in the Spirit of God does not permit us, however, the least intellectual and spiritual laziness. We must *use all the means which Providence puts today, as today, at our disposal,* in order to know better the man of today and the course of history, social processes and relations, and so on . . . Very often the Church has shown a defensive attitude, full of suspicion in regard to the behavioural sciences, whereas these are an indispensable instrument for the deepening of the knowledge of man. In a closed and static society the point of reference was constituted by the wisdom and prudence of the elders. Today this is no longer enough. Henceforth, the unrenounceable instruments are anthropology, the comparison of cultures, psychology, both individual and social, and also depth psychology. The Church cannot evangelize the world without making full use, obviously wise use, of the new sciences. The working-document for the preparation of the synod of 1974 rightly underlined that for an effective evangelization, it is necessary that the Church be present in focal points, where there are formed and where there arise conceptions and ideas on the world, on man and on history (cf. Part III, 1D). Nevertheless, in what follows, the document begins to accuse these sciences (anthropology, psychology, sociology) of characterizing a culture that ignores God and the gospel. It is necessary to ask whether this is a fair judgement or one which is too generalized. And in the cases where it is fair, would it not perhaps be better to attribute a part of the fault to Christians for not being actively present in these focal points of daily life? However, these sciences lose nothing of their importance; they

help us to understand better our culture and the actual historical moment, the dynamism of the social processes and the various inter-dependences between religion, family, economy, culture, politics and so on.

5. Already, according to St Thomas Aquinas, the degree of the virtue of discernment depends on a *connaturalitas* with truth and with good. The signs of the times are by their own nature an appeal to vigilance, to conversion and to the reform of structures. He who is not ready to unite personal conversion and renewal of structures in a single synthesis will never be able to discern and read the signs of the times.

This aspect should be stressed also in consideration of the fact that the theology and catechisms of the last decades have too unilaterally emphasized the *fides quae*, that is the content of revelation, and often in an excessively objective way. The biblical renewal and Christian existentialism have helped us to distinguish more clearly the importance of the *fides qua*, total openness and the gift of self, transcendence in listening, in receiving and in engaging one's self, without which the pure and simple content of the faith cannot be grasped. The content of faith does not bear fruit by itself. This is valid also for the discernment of the signs of the times: only the person and the community characterized by openness, by listening and by the prayer, 'Here I am, Lord, call me', are connatural with them.

6. Not only because of the waves of contestation and of prophetic protest, but also in order to understand the signs of the times, we must give the greatest attention to the *virtue of discernment* or of constructive criticism. Sour criticism and that of those who call everything in question without proposing a constructive plan on the other hand, and without having at the same time the will to engage deeply in personal conversion and in social reform, are useless and close the mind to authentic discernment.

7. For the connaturality so necessary for the discernment of the signs of the times, a great *hope* and profound confidence in God are indispensable. The pessimist and all those who are more confident in themselves than in God will never see the signs of the times in the right light. It is necessary that *first attention be given to the positive signs of the presence of God*. The Christian will not lose his time in useless lamentations

about 'bad days', but will look in the first place for what the Lord has done, what is his positive gift. The biblical approach speaks of the *kairos*, of the present moment, which offers us unrepeatable opportunities to do good, honouring thus the heavenly Father. For those who possess this openness full of confidence, even danger and temptation become a *kairos*, in the sense of a challenge received, in such a way that they do not permit themselves any more mediocrity, and decide for the following of Christ without reserve.

8. While exclusively human optimism conceals from itself, deceiving itself, the greatest dangers, the discernment of the signs of the times renders a person ready also for the criticism of idols and ideologies.[11] He who is sensitive to the signs of the presence of God becomes also capable of unmasking idols and ideologies, collective prejudices and false ideals. Today the criticism of ideologies has become a university discipline; this is also a reason not to renounce the use of such a new instrument. But, I repeat, a true criticism is not possible if persons and communities, including ecclesial ones, are not ready to accept prophetic contestation, and to open their eyes also to their own prejudices, idols and ideologies, and not only to note those of others.

5. *Watchfulness for the signs of the times becomes evangelization*

The first condition for evangelization is a profound and living faith. Faith is in the first place listening and openness, but also response and gift of self. A faith of this kind contains all the dynamics of witness and of commitment to the kingdom of God. The listening includes, necessarily, attention to the signs of the times; men and communities who do not want to give this attention inevitably bury God in the past. On the other hand, through personal and community watchfulness, people live in the presence of God, the Lord of history. Thus integrated in the whole of the proclamation of the gospel, the discernment of the signs of the times and their communication become evangelization, efficacious in the measure in which persons and communities are ready to give an existential response to these signs.

I shall attempt here to illustrate concretely the way in which the answer to the signs of the times becomes evangelization. I have chosen one of those which are actually most visible: the experience of the solidarity of mankind.

To give attention to this sign gives to the *Credo* a new mentality and a new spirit, without however adding anything to it.

— *We believe in one God, the Father, the Almighty*: we believe it in 'spirit and truth', in the measure in which we unite ourselves to all men without allowing ourselves to be scared or stopped by barriers erected by them. We believe in the one God and Father of all only if we respect in everyone his image, and try to develop in ourselves this image as a capacity to understand, to respect and to love every man.

— *Maker of all that is, seen and unseen*: we believe in him in as much as we use capacities and earthly goods, not only to our own advantage or that of our small group, but for the good of all.

— *We believe in one Lord, Jesus Christ, the only Son of God, eternally begotten of the Father . . . Through him all things were made*: we believe in this great mystery and we recognize truly the only begotten Son of God when we behave as his brothers and sisters. Christ manifests to us the Father by his works: the entire creation speaks of the Father, Jesus renders him visible to us as Love loving everyone. We adore the Father with him, in 'spirit and truth', if we listen to the invitation of creation and of history to unite solidly with the Son as brother of all.

— *For us men and for our salvation he came down from heaven: by the power of the Holy Spirit he became incarnate from the Virgin Mary, and was made man*: this, our faith, is sincere and becomes gratitude for the great gift made to us, if we become more human and commit ourselves to the eternal salvation of all, and, at the same time, to the promotion of the dignity of each person and, thus, of true solidarity.

— *For our sake he was crucified . . . he suffered death and was buried*: we believe in Christ, the humble Servant who has given his life to liberate man from the vicious circle of sin, if we try, with a combined and non-violent action, to overcome individual and collective egoisms, and to unite individuals, classes and peoples in a reciprocal respect.

— *On the third day he rose again . . . and is seated at the right hand of the Father*: we believe 'in spirit and truth' and we become witnesses of this gospel if we have confidence in the victory of generous love and of non-violence as expressions of solidarity and of engagement.

— *He will come again in glory to judge the living and the dead . . . and his kingdom will have no end*: this, our faith, is sincere and full of hope for the coming of Christ if we follow in the footsteps of the Lord who wanted to destroy all barriers, and who will judge everyone according to his commitment to an authentic fraternity, justice, peace and reconciliation.

— *We believe in the Holy Spirit, the Lord, the giver of life . . . He has spoken through the prophets*: we believe it and our faith becomes adoration of God 'in spirit and truth' if we use all our capacities, energy and charisms for the true solidarity of mankind. We contradict the law of the Spirit if we look for uniformity and unity imposed with violence and for the interests of a group. We are 'sacred liars' if, while confessing our faith in the Holy Spirit, who has spoken through prophets, we do not listen to their voice affirming and proclaiming that there is no salvation for humanity in this historical moment if we do not overcome collective egoisms and the politics of domination.

— *We believe in one holy catholic and apostolic Church*: this is true in the measure in which all of us, the people of God, become a visible and efficacious sign of our union with the Father, particularly through our engagement in bringing about the unity of all Christians in view of the unity of all people.

— *We acknowledge one baptism for the forgiveness of sins*: Christ was baptized not only in water but also in his blood, and through the Holy Spirit his baptism was a total gift of himself for the healing of men. We live according to our baptism which unites us to that of Christ, and we give thanks for the forgiveness of our sins in the measure in which we fight against injustices and against causes of separation among peoples and social classes, and work enthusiastically for universal reconciliation.

— *We look for the resurrection of the dead, and the life*

12

of the world to come: faith and hope unite here to invite us, extremely urgently, to use the present historical moment to commit ourselves to that solidarity and unity which brings us into a life of full fraternity and communion in God.

A community meditation such as this, which is, at the same time, mutual evangelization and preparation for witnessing in the world, cannot but include the humble admission of the distance between the faith fully lived and the striking imperfection of our witness. And it is precisely thus that common reflection turns into prayer: 'Lord, we believe: increase our faith; help us where our faith is falling short'.

6. *The universality and diversity of the signs of the times*

I now turn to concrete signs of the times particularly in relation to those phenomena which, both in their manner and their diverse intensity, concern the whole of humanity and each of its members. It is a matter of opportunities and values intimately experienced in a determinate historical moment. All the same, the diversity of cultures and of economic, social, cultural and political conditioning and so on do not permit a single and uniform approach to these signs, although they are common enough to the entire human race.

Evangelization should take account of what is more-or-less common and universal, and appeals to the vigilance of all and, at the same time, of what gives evidence of diversity in giving preference to one value or the other, in seeing the greater importance of one or the other, and in being more prepared for this or that opportunity. Certainly, the fact that the signs of the times have something which unites all permits a certain strategy of evangelization, but the diversity of these signs in various cultures and in different social groups excludes a precise codification of the signs of the times; it calls rather for a legislation which would be sufficiently sensitive to the multiplicity of mentalities and cultural, social and political structures and so on. The more all the basic communities, the local churches of a culture or of a continent, are united in the search for a concrete opportunity to enrich the universal dialogue of the entire Church, the more each of them will be able to discern the signs of the times. One of the signs of our times is undoubtedly social communication; it permits and leads to world dialogue. Thus it is that not only the local churches, but also the diverse religions and cultures, can and must enrich one another and correct themselves in turn, which fact does not mean that they must pursue conformism or, worse, syncretism; rather it demands, in fact, the contrary, a common search for truth, and unity in diversity. Another striking sign of our age is the call for equal rights for women in Church and society.

7. *Some of the principal signs of the times*

A. *Encouraging signs*

1. A new experience of *unity and solidarity* is today possible to mankind. In a manner unknown until now we are conscious of the fact that we are all in the same boat: either we liberate ourselves from the tendencies of violence and domination or this boat sinks. For the first time in history man is in a position where he can completely destroy the whole of mankind. But also, for the first time, he can reap from the multiple experiences and reflections of ancient cultures and those of today. Humanity can today unite itself through the use of its own genius and of all the resources and riches of this our earth and, perhaps soon, also of those of other planets.

All these new experiences and possibilities can and must become an integral part of evangelization, and they will if the great truths of faith manifest the more profound and true reasons for human solidarity and offer orientations and ends.[12] 'Here is found the specific contribution of the Church to civilizations: sharing the noblest aspirations of men, and suffering when she sees them not satisfied; she wishes to help them attain their full flowering. That is why she offers men what she possesses as her characteristic attributes: a universal vision of man and the human race.'[13]

2. While in Greek philosophy the concept of natural law recognized only the dignity of the Greek man, free and masculine, today there is in the whole world a great aspiration that *the equal dignity of all persons be recognized*. And

people of today are not satisfied with abstract principles: they want the dignity of all men and women to be recognized by all institutions, by all structures, and above all, by the concrete possibility that each person can express individual responsibility and co-responsibility in personal and social relations.

This sign of the times becomes evangelization if it is seen in the context of the good news that God has created man and woman in his image and likeness; he calls them to his friendship, while confiding to them the earth and the building of a fraternal society to the honour of the one Father. The dignity of each, in the diversity of gifts and capacities, becomes evangelization in the large vision of the Mystical Body of Christ (cf. 1 Cor 12). The demythologization and desacralization of many empty traditions and sacred things enters into the prophetic perspective of evangelization through the resacralization of the person in the human community and in the solidarity of salvation.

3. The very complex phenomenon of secularization and declericalization allows also a *demythologization of authority*. This does not mean that there is no more need for authority: it will, however, be conceived as service rendered to the community, so that all can grow in the knowledge of participation and co-responsibility. The same justice, in the perspective of the humanist and still more in that of the biblical 'new justice', demands that all search for good together in the articulation of co-responsibility.

This sign of the times becomes evangelization when the exercise of authority within the Church and at the vanguard gives testimony in the concrete to the concepts that I have expressed: humble service, subsidiarity, collegiality, co-responsibility.

4. The modern means of communication and other social processes have opened *the epoch of world-wide dialogue*. In order that this reality can be integrated and transformed into a vehicle of evangelization, the Church must deepen her knowledge of the new world, since man has become modified by this new state of things. Therefore, it is not so much a question of how the Church can use the technical means of communication and world-wide dialogue for evangelization; the fundamental question lies rather in the necessity that mentalities and ecclesiastical structures have the same wave-length. For example, the concept

of natural law should not contradict these new realities. For this reason a serious anthropological study and, inevitably, the comparing of various cultures, is indispensable, so that cultural conditioning, which has led to a too narrow concept of the natural law and, often, to an unacceptable ethico-juridical colonialism, can be unmasked. It is precisely this phenomenon which should be carefully examined and studied if moral theology wants to serve evangelization in an age of world-wide dialogue.

5. *The extremely dynamic character of our culture* will become an integral part of evangelization in the measure in which the Church becomes fully conscious of the new situation and discovers the authentic dynamism of the gospel and of the law of liberty and grace. Evangelization demands that the Church abandon not only out-dated juridical structures and certain styles of authority, but also insisting on unchangeable formulations of dogma and morals; she should abandon also too narrow cultural criteria and all the encrustations provoked by the attitude of self-defence. The Church receives from her Founder the power she needs only in so far as she unites herself with her message in the dynamics of the actual epoch.

6. The new sensitivity of the social *élites*, which progressively diffuses itself also among the masses, through a *sincerity of conscience in the search for the truth*, in respect for the liberty of consciences, becomes part of evangelization if the Church renounces all systems of control, promotion, threats and enticement and also renounces a concept of obedience which could compromise the sincerity of consciences and, thus, the credibility of the Church. If her life, her style of obedience and all her evangelization serve in the greatest degree to produce sensitive consciences, the Church can be a witness of the gospel to the new world and to those sections of humanity which will be decisive in the future.

The Church will already have made a great gain if she tries courageously to translate into active life the declarations of the Second Vatican Council on *religious freedom and conscience.* However, we cannot hide the fact that this concerns a very profound change which demands a rigorous examination of the collective conscience. In the Churches of the empire, of the state and of the masses, often conscience not only failed to find support but was even on the contrary deadened, and sometimes replaced by an obedience which remained at a pre-moral and pre-religious level. The whole of evangelization has to be re-thought in relation to the new presence of the Church as a minority, as the salt of the earth. For example, it will no longer be possible to make the concept of the sacramentality of marriage and the obligation to the ecclesiastical form (under pain of invalidity) depend uniquely on the baptismal register. A Church which assumes as a fundamental criterion only the external rite and cold statistics instead of the sincere faith of the person cannot evangelize the world of tomorrow.

7. For the rest it is sufficient to confront the classical treatment of the manuals of the twentieth century with the ideas that enter gradually into ecclesiastical documents and which characterize the great social movements of the world of today so as to be aware of how profound and general the re-thinking of all evangelization and particularly of moral theology must be, so that the Church can announce the gospel to the *new world which is hungry and thirsty for justice*, and feel that all have the right to *human advancement*,[14] to integral development, to decolonization and to authentic peace. The confrontation of the way in which social justice, and also international justice, is conceived today with the biblical concept of 'justification through grace alone' and of 'the new justice' brought by Christ, could become a great asset to and event of evangelization in the deepest and most total sense.

8. The enormous progress of the sciences and of technology and especially the process of secularization and desacralization have brought a *new consciousness of liberty and liberation.* Most of the things and situations which the man of yesterday accepted as divinely willed and inevitable have turned out malleable to the man of today. He becomes conscious that he can and must free himself from many encrustations and many conditionings. He knows the immense power of public opinion: each one can therefore understand that he is bound by the obligation to insert himself attentively and intelligently into public opinion, proposing convincing motives, through the means which permit the formation of a spiritually sound

climate, in his immediate surroundings and in world-wide dialogue.

Mankind begins to feel with an ever greater clarity that there are no immanent laws that will automatically guarantee human development. An authentic development is possible only in a courageous and serene confrontation of the situation of conflict. The key word can no longer be 'development' alone, but *'liberation*[15] *and development' together*. All this enters into the sweep of evangelization if moral theology would return to the wide Pauline vision of the *liberty of the children of God* under the law of grace and of *reconciliation*.[16]

9. In the perspective of the evangelization of the contemporary world, the sign of the times that is perhaps most important is the *change of the centres of influence from the old western world to the so-called 'third-world'*. By the year 2000, Asia, Latin America and Africa will have at least eighty per cent of the world's population — and this eighty per cent will be young — and these countries will be exercising therefore a determinate influence on the old western world itself. If the Church knows how to read the signs of the times and to respond to them properly, this phenomenon could become a true liberation from her unhappy ties with past European cultures, ties which have often been a great obstacle to the missions and which could even be very bad for the evangelization of coming generations of the western world. The Church is thus called and stimulated to recognize and to value every horizon of her catholicity and ecumenicity. This phenomenon should be decisive for the present theme.

B. *The challenge of alarming signs*

Up to this point I have underlined almost exclusively those signs of the times which open positively new horizons and indicate the presence of God, Creator and Redeemer, in the world. But if it is necessary to know how to see with an even greater clarity these signs, hope does not allow us to close our eyes to the dangers, to the signs of the presence of sin. But even these dangers, these signs of sin in the world, should be transformed into a challenge. And fully accepting this challenge we can think of the biblical concept of the 'kairos of temptation' (cf. Lk 8 : 13).

18

1. In the first place I am thinking of the new *idols* of success in exclusively economic development, of the power which leads from this to class distinctions and rich nations, and of the exploitation of sex.[17] These new idols become a saving challenge if Christians react with understanding of the absolutely central importance of the adoration of God 'in spirit and truth'. The new idols and ideologies can be unmasked and denounced only by those persons and communities who know how to pray, in the evangelical sense, and who, watching for the signs of the times, are ready to take the continuing glory of the Father as the golden thread of their own lives.

2. The world of today is deeply marked by *new differences*, polarizations and conflicts, both in the secular city and in the Church. These tensions have this time assumed a world-wide dimension and challenge Christians to discover all the dimensions of suffering in the light of the cross and reconciliation, which is surely not only a gratuitous gift of God but also a duty of every disciple of Christ.

3. The widely felt phenomenon of the *pollution of air and water* and the entire *human environment*, together with the damage caused to human resources by a rich and powerful minority, is a challenge which can not only arouse the co-responsibility of all, but even lead to salvation if, through it, Christians could discover fully the cosmic aspect of redemption.

4. The lack of readiness on the part of rich and powerful classes and nations *to renounce their own privileges and their domination*, must constitute for the Church a challenge to re-think her entire life, especially the exercises of authority, to bring it into the light of Christ the servant, in the spirit of the Magnificat lived by Mary.[18] Only a Church which has decided to live according to the sermon on the mount can be a gospel of liberation for a world threatened by the violence of the powerful and by the reaction, also equally violent, of the oppressed.

5. One of the most unhappy aspects of life today is *materialism*, whether it be incarnate in the capitalist system or in the various systems founded on dialectical materialism. This should be for Christians a pressing invitation to live the consciousness of God more intensively, in reflection and contemplation.

6. The most burning question in the world today is, however, *atheism*, and the diffusion of secularism. In my book, *Sin in the Secular Age*, I have tried to answer the challenge coming from this phenomenon with a re-thinking of the meaning of sin; here I shall seek to consider the fundamental lines of morals in the perspective of evangelization in respect to this same atheism and secularism in as much as it challenges Christians to give and witness more authentically to their message of salvation and love.

NOTES

1 Cf. J. Galot, 'Che cosa significa evangelizzazione?', in *Civiltà Cattolica*, 1973, III, pp. 105–116; Synod of bishops, *The evangelization of the modern world*, Vatican City, 1973; Italian Episcopal Conference, *Evangelizzazione e sacramenti*, Pastoral document of the Italian bishops, Rome, July 12, 1973; D. Grasso, 'Evangelizza-zione Oggi', in *Civiltà Cattolica*, 1973, II, 451–459, and 'Pre-evangelizzazione o evangelizzazione?', in *Rivista del Clero Italiano*, 14 (1973), pp. 527–532.

2 Cf. B. Häring, *Macht und Ohnmacht der Religion*, Salzburg, Otto Müller, 1956; J.B. Metz, 'Political theology', in *Sacramentum Mundi*, Vol. 5, London, Burns and Oates, 1969; Metz, Moltmann, Oelmueller, *Kirche im Prozess der Aufklärung*, Munich, 1970; J. Paupert, *Perspectives de théologie politique*, Toulouse, 1969; H.B. Meyer, *Politik im Gottesdienst*, Innsbruck, 1971; J. Bommer, 'Verkündigung als gesellschaftskritischer *Vorgang*', in *Diakonia* 4 (1973), pp. 293–302; E. Bethge, 'Politik ohne Kirche, Kirche ohne Politik', in *Evangelische Theologie* 32 (1972), pp. 579–594; B. Sorge, 'Evangelizzazione e impegno politico, in *Civiltà Cattolica*, 1973, IV, pp. 7–25.

3 Cf. *Theological Dictionary of the New Testament* (Edited by Kittel).

4 Cf. J. Alfaro, *Reflexions à l'occasion du douzième anniversaire de l'enc. 'Pacem in Terris' du Pape Jean XXIII*, Vatican City, 1973.

5 Cf. J. Jeremias, *Die Gleichnisse Jesu*, Göttingen, 1965; W. Pannenberg, *Theologie und Reich Gottes*, Gütersloh, 1971.

6 Cf. B. Häring, *A Theology of Protest*, New York, Farrar, Strauss & Giroux, 1970, pp. 21–38; M.D. Chenu, 'Prophets et theologiens dans l'Eglise', in *Masses Ouvrière*, Oct. 1963; 'Un peuple prophétique', in *Esprit* 35 (1967).

7 Cf. B. Häring, *Morality is for Persons*, New York, 1971, pp. 104–114.

8 The concept of natural law and the history of salvation must be reconsidered in this perspective. Cf. B. Häring, *Morality is for Persons*.

9 M.D. Chenu, *L'Evangile dans le temps*, Paris 1964; 'Les signes des temps', in *Nouvelle Revue Théologique*, 1965, 29–44; 'Les signes des temps: reflections théologiques', in *L'Eglise dans le monde de ce temps*, II, Paris, 1967, 191–194.

10 Cf. B. Häring, 'Prayer in a secular age', *Faith and Morality in a Secular Age*, St Paul Publications, Slough, 1973, pp. 200–226.

11 Cf. B. Häring, *Sin in the Secular Age*, Slough, 1974, pp. 89–90; J. Habermas, *Technik und Wissenschaft als Ideologie*, Frankfurt, 1968; *Erkenntnis und Interesse*, Frankfurt, 1968; B. Badura, *Sprachbarrieren: zur Zoziologie der Kommunika-tion*, Stuttgart, 1971; R. Zerfass, 'Herrschaftsfreie Kommunikatioeine Forderung an die Kirchliche Verkündigung?', in *Diakonia* 4 (1973), pp. 339–350.

12 Cf. E. Lange, 'The Test Case of Faith', in *The Ecumenical Review*, 25 (1973),

pp. 270–285; *Die ökumenische Utopie, oder was bewegt die ökumenische Bewegung?* — *am Biespiel Löwen 1971: Menscheneinheit-Kircheneinheit,* Kreuz Verlag, Stuttgart, 1973.

13 Paul VI, *Octogesima Adveniens,* n. 40 Cf. *Evangelii nuntiandi* nos. 37–38.

14 Cf. Paul VI, *Evangelii nuntiandi* nos. 30–32.

15 Synod of bishops, 1971, *Document on justice in the world,* nos. 6, 37; Chr. Hampe, *Die Autorität der Freiheit,* 3 vols., Munich, 1967; M. Raske, K. Schäfer, N. Wetzel, *Eine freie Kirche fur eine freie Welt,* Dusseldorf, 1969; K. Rahner, *Libertà e manipolazione nella Chiesa e nella Società,* Bologna, 1971; L. Hoffmann, *Auswege aus der Sackgasse,* Munich, 1971.

16 Cf. E. Castro, 'Conflict and Reconciliation', *The Ecumenical Review* (25 1973), pp. 286–294.

17 Cf. B. Häring, *Sin in the Secular Age,* St Paul Publications, Slough, 1974, p. 94, pp. 134–168.

18 Cf. B. Häring, *The Song of the Servant, Biblical Meditations on Mary the Mother and Model of the Church,* St Paul Publications, Slough, 1977.

PART TWO

THE MORALS OF EVANGELIZATION AND
THE EVANGELIZATION OF MORALS

After these general reflections on the basis of the whole of moral theology in relation to evangelization, I must face a series of urgent problems on the role of morals in the evangelization of the world of today. One can speak of a morality of evangelization: not only must the moral message be radically subordinate to evangelization, but it must also be seen that there are moral laws inherent in evangelization itself. First of all we accept the gospel as *the law*: we can, we must and we want to live the gospel and bring it to the ends of the earth. In the first place we can speak of a scale of values which indicates the priority of the gospel over moral norms, of grace over moral imperatives, of the kingdom of God over human needs. The more moral theology depends on the gospel the more it becomes itself evangelized and makes transparent the saving presence of God. If we recognize the priority of the gospel and evangelization over moral imperatives we shall free ourselves from that moralism which makes itself impenetrable to grace and which has often been an obstacle to the joy of the gospel and the evangelization of other cultures and of new generations.

1

The morality of evangelization

'It would be misery to me not to preach (the gospel)' (1 Cor 9 : 16): this is true not only for Paul, but for the whole Church. A terrible 'woe' fell from the lips of the Lord upon the scribes and Pharisees who, because of their 'justice according to the law' (that is, moralism), would close their heart to the gospel, searching also to prevent others from entering into the kingdom of God (cf. Lk 11 : 52). Our salvation depends on the joyous and grateful acceptance that we accord the gospel and on the will to translate the joyful news into practice, and it is not possible to accept the gospel sincerely without becoming ambassadors and messengers of its reconciliation.

1. *Evangelization and the Eucharist*

The fact of having been gratuitously reconciled became for Paul the most urgent motive for preaching the gospel (cf. 1 Cor 9 : 18; 2 Cor 11 : 7; Mt 10 : 8). The unmerited love shown to us by Christ impels us to put ourselves at the service of the gospel of reconciliation (cf. 2 Cor 5 : 14–20). To recognize the gratuity of the gift of salvation and of reconciliation transforms all our life into a Eucharist, into a thanksgiving; and thus we become, by an internal necessity, messengers and propagators of the joyful news of the gospel of peace.

Christ, the living gospel of the Father, lived this Eucharist. The fundamental characteristic of Jesus, from the first instant of his human consciousness, is the quick readiness to be the servant of the gospel, the living revelation of the Father. The whole life of the Lord is thanksgiving to God who has revealed to him, his humble servant, the fullness of his mystery. 'I thank thee, Father, Lord of heaven and earth, for hiding these things from the learned and wise, and revealing them to the simple. Yes, Father, such was thy choice . . . . Everything is entrusted to me by my Father; and no one knows who the Son is but the Father, or who the Father is but the Son and those to whom the Son may choose to reveal him' (Lk 10:21–22). He who has received the fullness of sonship and of the Spirit commits his entire life and death to communicating to us the joyful news. 'Let us go on to the country towns in the neighbourhood; I have to proclaim my message there also; that is what I have come to do' (Mk 1:38).

The evangelizing mission of the Church issues from the Eucharist in which Christ himself continues to proclaim his incarnation, death, resurrection and ascension to heaven. There he unites us to his thanksgiving to the Father and to his evangelization which springs from gratitude.

Christ, the living Word, the Word of the Father incarnate, is the great Sacrament which, with the message of salvation, communicates also grace and life. Christ is at the same time the acting and faithful Word and the witness to it. Faith is the positive and grateful response to the Word which gives us life; its culmination is in the celebration of the sacraments, which are the reception of the vivifying Word in an adherence which becomes of necessity the coherent testimony of Christian life (cf. *Ad gentes*, 5). The word and testimony of Christ render the love of the Father visible; this reality touches us in the sacraments and transforms us, the people of God, the disciples of Jesus, into visible signs of the gospel; and the more our lives are transformed by it the more we shall be capable, by divine grace, of celebrating the Eucharist and the other sacraments in a spirit of gratitude.

The document of the Italian Episcopal Conference on the 'Sacraments and evangelization' gives a good indication of this process of evangelization: '— from the word, to the sacrament, to the new life: this is the dynamics of Christian existence, which in order to conserve and develop itself must begin over and over again at the sources themselves from which it has issued, returning from life to the sacrament, to the word.'[1] Christ does not only renew in us and with us the memorial of his death and resurrection but also unites us with his thanksgiving to the Father, and such action cannot fail to become urgent for the preaching of the joyful news to all men.

I completely agree with Marcel Légaut when he affirms that

the future of Christianity and especially of the evangelization of the world depends fundamentally on the capacity of the disciples of Christ to celebrate the Eucharistic memorial.[2]

The Church which finds its centre of life and mission in the Eucharist, and which knows how to celebrate it, will not be seen so much as an institution preoccupied with its own conservation, but rather as 'an expedition in the name of Christ to the very ends of the earth'.[3] He who celebrates and lives the Eucharist becomes, in Christ, a living gospel. His eschatological hope and his invocation *marana-tha* ('Come, Lord Jesus') become mission through the communication of this hope and of this desire to all nations.

2. *The Lordship of Jesus Christ*

The principal reason which moves us to evangelize the whole world is not morals in itself, because there is no Christian morals without the newness and integral uniqueness of Christ. Christ is not a Prophet to be put beside Isaiah, Buddha, Confucius or Mohammed. Christ is *the* Prophet, the ultimate and definitive word of the Father to the world. He is *the* eternal Word, the Son who is in the bosom of the Father, who has come and was made man so that we could know the Father. 'This is eternal life: to know thee who alone art truly God, and Jesus Christ whom thou hast sent' (Jn 17 : 3). The true development of humanity comes from the explicit knowledge of Christ. 'He is the image of the invisible God; the first-born of all creation; for in him all things were created, in heaven and on earth, visible and invisible . . . all things were created through him and for him. He is before all things and in him all things hold together' (Col 1 : 15–17). The person who has not arrived at faith in Christ does not yet have full knowledge of the origin, of the centre and the scope of his own existence.

The diligent readiness for dialogue which aims at discovering what is good and true in the great non-Christian religions, should become a new and more important motive for making Christ, the unique Saviour, known; in fact, wherever there is something good, true or beautiful there is a presence of Christ, hidden or revealed, which must reach complete explicitation.

'Today the confession that, in contrast to the various aspirants to the monopoly of religious truth, it is Jesus who is the supreme authority should be proclaimed in the midst of a society which is dominated by the idea that every truth is relative and partial.'[4] The position of those Christians who no longer want to announce Christ as the unique Saviour, having found in other religions partial values, is not to be envied; because these values derive from Christ and carry in themselves the innate desire to be attributed to him. 'What is necessary today is an interpretation of the relationship between what God has accomplished in Jesus Christ and what acts in the complexes of human life.'[5]

Christ was made Servant. The Word of the Father descended from heaven as Man, for our salvation. We respond recognizing him in the Holy Spirit as Lord to the glory of the Father (cf. Rom 1 : 4; 10 : 9; 1 Cor 8 : 6; 12 : 3).

3. *The irrenounceable priority in the preaching of the gospel*

To want to reduce Christianity to a morality — and, worse, to a moralism — has disastrous consequences, for morality itself as well as for evangelization. Christ became man and came down from heaven for our salvation, but we cannot for this reason instrumentalize God and his only begotten Son. He brought us salvation through his absolute obedience to the Father; he announces to us the total future, and a more fraternal world, proclaiming, with his word and death, the kingdom of God. Man does not save himself if he adores God for the exclusive end of saving himself! The human race will not find salvation and authentic development if it would accept the kingdom of God only in as much as it wants its own salvation, sometimes for purely worldly ends. He who does not give glory to God builds himself on his own erroneous ideas of salvation, and will very soon ignore its eschatological dimensions; in this way he will become a slave to the transience of the present moment and of the immediate future, imprisoning religion also in his individual and collective egoism.

Emmanuel Kant fought against the ethics of self-perfection, because it does not recognize the majesty of good and truth in itself. But his thought does not reach ultimate conclusions, because his whole concept of religion is based on that of morals.[6] The best theologians, including those of the reformed Churches, have perceived clearly the great danger of a reduction of the gospel to a *Kulturchristentum* or a *social gospel*.[7] Such a danger is still greater today, and not only in the 'death of God' theology, but also in various forms, more or less dissimulated and masked, of the horizontalism which recognize the validity of religion only in so far as it subordinates itself to the ideas, sometimes ephemeral, of development, of revolution, of liberation or power.

Man, a sinner, will always be tempted, whether on the individual level or on the collective level, to subjugate the gospel to his own ideas and ends. It is therefore necessary that conscience should ask itself always, with a rigorous examination, if persons, communities and structures are truly at the service of the gospel. The gospel and evangelization have not the exaltation of the Church as their scope; rather, only when the Church is the servant of the joyful news is she truly holy and apostolic. If this absolute priority is not in evidence, new idols and new ideologies are created, and the result is the falsification of dogmatic and moral language itself.[8]

As we have seen, evangelization includes of necessity the call to justice, peace, reconciliation, fidelity and many other moral values. This call, however, should never try to become independent of the gospel, nor to assume the role of protagonist. The kingdom of God, the glory of God, who, through Christ in the Holy Spirit, manifests the splendour of his justice, his love, his mercy, should always occupy the first place. The dynamism of the moral demands of faith is strengthened and becomes more authentic when the Lordship of God in Christ is accepted in itself. The moral imperative retains its vigour and its identity only if it is founded on the indicative which proclaims the initiative of God, his grace and his kingdom, his reconciling action.

Let us therefore avoid using formulae of the kind of '*faith and works*': it is not good that faith and moral imperatives and human works should be placed side by side as additions. True evangelization is through faith which liberates us from egoism and which bears fruit in love and in justice, in mercy and in peace for the life of the world.

From what has been said it becomes clearer and clearer how urgent it is to recognize the priority of faith and of prayer as existential experience of the gospel, of the presence of God and of listening to God. Meditation on the word of God and joyous and living celebration of the mysteries of redemption must have the first place in the whole Church and, in a particular manner, among her ministers. In this way the specifically Christian character of morals will also be guaranteed.

The morality of evangelization will lie not only in the humility of the moralist but also in the humility of his system itself. The man who puts his confidence in the gospel will find the energy to live it and thus will understand that it is not in the first place at the service of the humanization of the world, but that, nevertheless, if it is received with humility, it will be the greatest humanizing force.[9]

It is true that faith cannot be living, joyful, and grateful without bearing fruit; but on the other hand it cannot bear abundant fruit when it is not a listening to and a total gift of man to the sovereignty of God. The *proprium* of Christian morals, if we want to be exact, is not the *humanum* as such, but the loving acceptance of the kingdom of God and of its springing from faith and eschatological hope; it is not love in itself, but the union of one's self to that love with which God, in Christ, loves the world so as to save it.

4. *Poverty in spirit as the condition of a living faith and authentic evangelization*

The typically Christian morality is that which springs from the paschal mysteries and expresses itself in the beatitudes, especially in the first: 'Blessed are those who know their need of God; the kingdom of Heaven is theirs' (Mt 5 : 3). We should not forget for one instant that the blessed poor man is Jesus himself who, through the Holy Spirit, became Servant and recognizes everything as the gift of the Father, giving himself back to him in the service of his brothers and sisters without return (cf. Jn 6 : 64). The Lord insisted on the fact that the message brought by him is not his but the Father's, 'for I have taught them all that I learned from thee, and they have received it: they know with certainty that I came from thee' (Jn 17 : 8). The communication of the Word, which is spirit and truth, is always an act of thanksgiving to the Father, 'I have called you friends, because I have disclosed to you everything that I heard from my Father' (Jn 15 : 15).

Humility and poverty in spirit signify existential gratitude for the fact that all is a gift of God; the only interest therefore is that God may be honoured and loved. The Church proclaims the gospel which convinces the world in as much as she follows Christ the Servant with Mary the handmaid. Ecclesiocentrism would be the greatest obstacle to evangelization. When the Church truly evangelizes she does not place her confidence in herself. The disciples of the Lord who are dedicated to the gospel, individually or in community, may never claim to bring a superior culture. They recognize that there would be no greater sacrilege than the one accomplished by making the mission of evangelization the instrument of a culture, whatever that culture may be, even if it be Latin. The apostle is all things to all men: Hebrew to the Hebrews, Greek to the Greeks, and not for any vain strategy! The Church cannot be a boastful museum of multiple treasures of the past, especially if this is to the detriment of her evangelizing mission, which can develop with a spirit of humility and of simplicity only through actual cultures.

The Church will renounce every privilege even justly acquired, when this privilege could disrupt evangelization or even compromise credibility (cf. *Gaudium et spes,* 76). She will not fortify herself with a uniform law and with centralistic controls where that could conceal the testimony of the Emmanuel, always near to every culture and at every age. He who dedicates himself to evangelization should always do so as a humble servant, never as one who dominates. 'The apostles, their successors, and those who assist these successors have been sent to announce to men Christ, the Saviour of the world. Hence in the exercise of their apostolate they must depend on the power of God, who very often reveals the might of the gospel through the weakness of its witnesses. For those who dedicate themselves to the ministry of God's word should use means and helps proper to the gospel. In many respects these differ from the supports of the earthly city' (*Gaudium et spes,* 76).

It is undeniable that it is a question of an extremely demanding programme, both for persons and for the structures of the Church.

The Church admits and accepts the Lordship of God and the gratuity of reconciliation through the confession of her sins, whether this concerns personal acts or the alienation of structures and institutions and centres of ecclesiastical power: only such a confession, frank and serene, can fill the gap between the ideal of the gospel and the inadequacy of the evangelizer. A Church in a perennial state of vigilant self-defence or a prevalently apologetic theology leads inevitably to ideology.

If the Church distributes presents from the rich and forms an alliance with the powerful and dominating so as to receive alms from them, even if it be to pass these on to the poor, she is not on the wave length of the gospel; she must re-tune herself in humility, conscious of her poverty and grateful for the divine forbearance. Only when she confesses with her whole life that God is sufficient for her and renounces the means used by the powers of the world, only then does she become an evangelizing agent.

The Church can affirm her substantial infallibility, only admitting that she has made mistakes, even officially, so many times, because she has been compromised by declarations in fields in which she had no competence and has adopted for herself earthly power which was forbidden her by the Lord himself. She is humble in spirit if she does not offer certainties when she is not sure that they come either from revelation or from common reflection and experience before God. She is humble if she accepts the provisory nature of so many things giving thanks to the Lord of certainty in the essential truth of faith.

The Church can preach the gospel when her only intention is to be faithful, and not to acquire importance in the world.

The Church evangelizes if each one is satisfied with his own charism, happy to co-operate with all: the various competences and qualities become united therefore in discrete and disinterested service.

The spreading of the gospel of Christ who, 'came not to be served, but to serve', can be the work only of humble servants; and therefore the evangelizers cannot participate in oppressive political structures, but must turn their mission into cordial fraternity, and the more they feel their own insufficiency the more powerful the grace of Christ makes people. 'Where the love of God reigns no one wants any more to dominate over others; there is created an ambience free from domination: people accept each other in turn, pardon each other, carry each other's burdens. There also they celebrate and rejoice together and there also is constituted a space where all that has become, in Christ, saving event can become present witness.'[10] Where the disciples of Christ accept without reserve, in themselves, the kingdom of God, the opposition between dominators and dominated is overcome because the desire of domination ceases.[11] In a world stubbornly opposed to feudalism and to absolutism it becomes ever more evident that the Church cannot be present as a diplomatic or political force: a style strange to the humility of the gospel and to the best forms of the exercise of authority today should be absolutely excluded. The most humble messengers will be the messengers most adapted to the kingdom of Christ the Servant and to the Father; that is, in evangelization those will be first who feel and comfort themselves as last.

Christ gave to his Church the ministry of the apostles as a teaching college. This is not to serve primarily for the control of orthodoxy, but for the convincing communication of the joyful news: such a demand should condition the whole style of the exercise of the magisterial authority.

5. *The absolute novelty of the gospel and the novelty of the moral life in Christ*

Christ is personified joyful news; he is unsurpassable and permanent novelty. Faith and evangelization are always an experience of novelty.[12] In a certain sense one can say that the whole history of the world is a desire to see Christ as the fulfilment of that which existed already and exists, but also as the new beginning and the absolute future. 'I tell you, many prophets and kings wished to see what you now see, yet never saw it' (Lk 10 : 24). He who receives Christ, the living gospel, experiences, with the renewal accomplished by the Spirit, the novelty of the saving message. But the absolute novelty of the experience of faith cannot be proclaimed ignoring or neglecting the novelty of the moral life. The kingdom of God is given to us together with the gift of the Spirit which renews our hearts and the face of the earth; from this gift comes a constant appeal: 'be converted, and believe the gospel' (Mk 1 : 14). The gospel of Christ, full revelation of the life and love of the Father, also brings us a new life, *the life in Christ*.

It is always a question of the novelty with which the love of the Father is revealed in the Son and through the Holy Spirit. 'God loved the world so much that he gave his only Son' (Jn 3 : 16). The motive and the measure of love are therefore new: 'I give you a new commandment: love one another as I have loved you' (Jn 13 : 34; 15 : 12). Only in a continuous process of conversion of the heart and renewal of the entire life, will Christians experience and be able to communicate the novelty of 'the life-giving law of the Spirit in Christ Jesus' (Rom 8 : 2). The disciples sent to spread the good news carry in themselves the law through the new life in Christ, given them by the Spirit (cf. 1 Cor 1 : 29). In the preaching of the Apostle of the Gentiles this baffling and marvellous novelty of the love of God and the law of the Spirit occupied a place absolutely central and dominant. It is, in fact, the novelty of the paschal mystery of Christ, humble servant, exalted by the Father as Lord, who gives us a share in his life. 'The life I now live is not my life, but the life which Christ lives in me; and my present bodily life is lived by faith in the Son of God, who loved me and gave himself up for me' (Gal 2 : 20). 'And live in love as Christ loved you' (Eph 5 : 2).

Paul saw the novelty and its experience threatened by the tendency of the nomists to impose prejudicially customs, laws and juridical norms. And also he was not afraid in the least to challenge the confidence that the Greeks put in their wisdom. He wanted to preach to them, 'without relying on the language of worldly wisdom, so that the fact of Christ on his cross might have its full weight' (1 Cor 1 : 17). On the other hand the apostle adapted himself to the environment and the cultures in which he preached the good news, and this, in order not to obscure the novelty of the message by confusing it with foreign and superfluous elements.

A great difficulty for the spreading of the Christian message among all peoples comes from the danger of confounding or mixing up our *ethos*, historically conditioned, with the firm and essential exigences of Christianity.[13]

There is no necessity to bring to the cultures inspired by the magnificent morals of Confucianism the Aristotelian or Stoic ethics. We can admit without difficulty that the moral teaching of Confucius is superior to many western ethical systems. Imposing the morals of Christ in the clothing of western categories, we risk completely covering the novelty of the gospel and of the new life. We can on the contrary accept and appreciate all the good and beauty that is present in the great moral religions of Asia. The novelty of the gospel and of the life of Christ thus maintains its freshness unchanged.

We westerners — marked as we are by technology, by organization, by confidence in material progress — cannot communicate the gospel to the profoundly religious people of Asia and Africa if we do not live the novelty of the prayer taught us by the Lord and if we do not transform such life into the fruit of contemplation of the Word incarnate.

We can and we must, certainly, appraise the values and the moral sense of humanism, but we shall be able to unmask the traps of human self-sufficiency only by adoring in spirit and truth and living that morality which springs from faith and flowers in gratitude for the unmerited grace of God.

And since the faith is not an ideology to put beside so many others, we shall be in a position to communicate the novelty of the gospel and of its morality only in the measure in which the experience of faith has deepened in us the joy, the gratitude, and the knowledge of Christ and of the Father and his design for all people. It follows evidently, therefore, that the evangelization of the world demands first of all the spirit of authentic prayer and meditation on the gospel, never however separated from readiness for the existential translation of the word meditated.

6. *The evangelization confided to the ecclesial community*

The Church's reason for being is the continuous praise of God and the proclamation of the gospel to all nations. Christ wanted a visible Church, united in faith, in hope and in charity by the Holy Spirit, so that through her the solidarity of his salvation and his testimony could take root in human history. The gospel was not confided to a single apostle, but to the entire community of disciples. These had to fulfil their mission as a community, witnessing by its unity and love. 'But it is not for these alone that I pray, but for those also who through their words put their faith in me; may they all be one: as thou, Father, art in me, and I in thee, so also may they be in us, that the world may believe that thou didst send me' (Jn 17 : 20-21).

To evangelize the world it is indispensable that we experience the sacraments as visible and efficacious signs of the unity of the people of God. The sacraments, especially baptism, the Eucharist and reconciliation (penance), are a perennial mission whose end is to make the gospel present through solidarity and unity in Christ. Only in the measure in which we are united in Christ with one faith and with one hope, in love and in reciprocal pardon, do we have the infallible and at the same time communicable experience that God is the Father of all and Christ is the man for every other. Evangelization is, in essence, an event of the believing and adoring community.

The mission to evangelize the entire world is given to the Church through the gift of the Spirit which works in all, through all, and in view of all. It therefore has its presupposition in the appreciation of the diverse gifts, ministries, works and charisms of the Spirit. 'There are varieties of gifts, but the same Spirit. There are varieties of service, but the same Lord. There are many forms of work, but all of them, in all, are the work of the same God' (1 Cor 12 : 4-6). If we are docile and grateful, the diversity of gifts is a testimony of the one faith. The Church has so much need of knowledge and of wisdom, of the gift of healing, of that which increases social works as an expression of charity, of apostles constituted to govern and to teach officially, of prophets who shake the false security of all, including authority; but she is in need above all of charity which becomes the ministry of reconciliation and proof of the presence of Christ (cf. 1 Cor 12-13).

The self-understanding of the Church manifested by the Second Vatican Council stresses the mission which is proper to her as the messianic people, to be a sign, practically a sacrament of union with God and of union with mankind. Lay persons also have their charisms and participate fully in the mission of the Church and in the prophetic and priestly roles of Christ the Servant (cf. *Lumen gentium*, 30–38). The evangelization of the world today and that of tomorrow depends above all on the translation into practice of what the Council has taught, especially regarding collegiality and subsidiarity as important structures of the Church.

If Christians could truly become adorers of the one Father in the Son through the one Spirit, then they would be united even in the diversity of cultures and of charisms. The first duty of evangelization is to recall with force the whole of Christianity so that it may be converted to organic unity; the ecumenical movement is an irrenounceable part of this evangelization. If the only interest of Christians is the glory of God and sensitiveness to his kingdom of grace and truth, they will find the courage to confess their sins against unity and to recognize the good and the truth in other ecclesial communities.

One of the great obstacles which intervened to disrupt unity was the erroneous concept of teaching authority in the different churches, which put the primary emphasis on the self-defence of the doctrinal formulations instead of uniting all the energy in the vital communication of the saving truth to humanity. If all Christians are stimulated and moved to share the fullness of the gospel with every social class, culture and generation they will understand more easily that diversity of formulas does not necessarily indicate an opposition; rather it can guarantee complementarity in evangelization.

If orthodoxy is conceived, measured and seen in the great perspective of evangelization and of witness it will be easier to overcome those heterodox orthodoxies which have marked so many dogmatic formulas, imposed by those who did not truly live the gospel to its depths. It is not possible to evangelize the world through an orthopraxis which gives little attention to evangelical truth. We are however sincerely preoccupied with this truth only if the saving message is communicated in the witnessing of unity and confession of our sins, individual as well as collective. An ecumenism which is concerned only with

the social obligation to development and liberation from oppressing structures is not sufficient: its centre should be the
anxiety to communicate the authentic message of Christ
credibly and effectively to all people, in mutual charity.

Ecumenism signifies experiences of the gratuity of the reconciliation which comes to us from God. Grateful, therefore, for
the gift of reconciliation, the diverse ecclesial communities,
both their people and their authorities, will be humble and
generous, will let themselves be liberated from self-defence and
from that erroneous or exaggerated apologetics which in the
past have sterilized the message of salvation, dividing
Christians.

Ecumenism signifies readiness to consider the history of
Christianity, with its virtues and sins, as a common history,
to praise God together for his mercy and pardon and to learn
from both the positive testimony and the sins of the past. One
of the causes of schisms and strifes was precisely the lack of
poverty and humility in ecclesial institutions and in those who
were constituted in authority. Evangelization of the world
demands humility even at the institutional level, and poverty
is its condition as is also the humility of Christians.[14]

7. *Evangelization and pre-evangelization*

In the last decades much has been written and discussed concerning pre-evangelization.[15] Evangelization is the explicit
proclamation of the mystery of Christ and a direct invitation
to adhere to his gospel; it is expressed in *parrhesia* (courageous
confidence), in frankness of word and of witness on the part
of persons and of communities which manifest the priority of
the gospel and of the new life of Christ; evangelization is present wherever the Church shows herself, in whatever structure
or institution, a humble handmaid of the gospel.

What prepares more or less directly for evangelization can
be called pre-evangelization. Thus the activity of Christians
who dedicate themselves either to social, or charitable works,
or to the instruction and the spreading of culture can be pre-
evangelization in the measure in which these are inspired by

the love which the gospel teaches us and by solicitude that all may know the love of God revealed in Christ.

Dialogue concerned with moral values — justice, peace, liberation, co-responsibility, and so on — and on the subject of the natural law inscribed in the hearts of men can be pre-evangelization if those who sustain and witness to moral commitment are completely inspired and motivated by the gospel and constantly attentive for the moment of grace in which it will be possible to speak directly of the gospel.[16]

Pre-evangelization can be conducted only by those who are deeply permeated by the gospel and convinced of the priority of the kingdom of God over any social or moral work whatever and over every purely human value.

It is clear therefore, that under the term pre-evangelization we can easily find idols and ideologies hidden. For example, one thinks of those who maintain that making underdeveloped people literate, the turning of nomads into cultivators, technical progress, social organization, the adoption of certain political systems are more urgent than evangelization and are a condition of it. People who think in this way are surely still prisoners of their culture transformed into an idol. In the same category are those who think they must first teach a certain philosophy, a determined ethical system or a certain theory of laws or of natural law: they hide the gospel and have not yet been liberated by it and through it.

Those who believe they must evangelize especially in the direction of moral virtue, of doctrines and social and political engagement are always easy victims to Pelagianism, that is, they run the risk of giving the first place to works, thus practically neglecting the kingdom of grace of Christ crucified and risen.

A commitment to peace and justice can be pre-evangelization if it is exercised for the good *of all*; but if it becomes a taking of a unilateral position for the support of a group or a class, then it becomes a form of polytheism, [17] and can never be pre-evangelization, because it lacks the foundation of authentic testimony.

A commitment to and a discussion of moral and religious values are pre-evangelization and they express the *analogia fidei* in the proportion in which the search for the true and the good is sincere and occupies the first place. If such a search is relegated to second place, overwhelmed by the pursuit of honours, successes and careers, it becomes practical polytheism. Values and moral virtues are not pre-evangelization in themselves, but only if they are inspired by grace and lived for the honour of God.

NOTES

1 Italian Episcopal Conference, *Evangelizzazione e sacramenti*, Roma, 1973, n. 5.
2 Cf. M. Legaut, *Introduction à l'intelligence du passé et de l'avenir du Christianisme*, Paris, 1970, pp. 290–370; C. Bonicelli, 'Dopo l'inchiesta nazionale Evangelizzazione e Sacramenti', in *Rivista del Clero Italiano* 54 (1973) pp. 647–651.
3 L. Newbigin, *La Chiesa missionaria nel mondo di oggi*, Roma, 1968, p. 11; Cf. N.P. Moritzen, *Die Kirche als Missio*, Wuppertal, 1968; J. Schütte (ed.), *Mission nach dem Konzil*, Mainz, 1967.
4 L. Newbigin, *op. cit.*, p. 23.
5 *Ibid.*, p. 39.
6 Cf. B. Häring, *Il sacro e il bene*, Brescia, 1968, pp. 108–132.
7 Cf. H.R. Niebuhr, *Pious and Secular America*, New York, 1958; *Christ and Culture*, New York, 1956; *Radical Monotheism and Western Culture*, New York, 1960; P. Ramsey, *Faith and Ethics*, New York, 1965.
8 Cf. E. Schillebeeckx, 'The crisis in the language of faith as a hermeneutical problem', in *Concilium* 5 (1973), pp. 31–45.
9 Yet without doubt it can be said that evangelical morals is at the service of man and therefore pays attention specifically to the *humanum*. Cf. J. Gründel, F. Rauh, V. Eid, *Humanum: Moral-theologie im Dienst des Menschen*, Köln, 1972.
10 R. Zerfass, 'Herrschaftsfreie Kommunikation: eine Forderung an die Kirchliche Verkündigung?', in *Diakonia* 4 (1973), p. 343; Cf. R. Zerfass, *Der Streit um die Laienpredigt*, Freiburg, 1973; J. Habermas, *Erkenntnis und Interesse*, Frankfurt, 1973; B. Badura, *Sprachbarrieren: zur Soziologie der Kommunikation*, Stuttgart, 1971; H.E. Bahr, *Verkündigung: zur öffentlichen Kommunikation in der demokratischen Gesellschaft*, Hamburg, 1968; H.D. Bastion, *Theologie der Frage: jdeen zur Grundlegung einer theologischen Dialektik und zur Kommunikation der Kirche in der Gegenwart*, Munich, 1969; G. Baum, *Glaubwürdogkeit: zum Selbstverständis der Kirche*, Freiburg, 1969; M. Raske, K. Schäfer, N. Wetzel (ed.), *Eine freie Welt*, Düsseldorf, 1969; L. Hoffmann, *Auswege aus der Sackgasse*, Munich, 1971; K. Rahner, *Libertà e manipolazione nella Chiesa e nella società*, Bologna, 1971.
11 W. Pannerberg, 'Geschichtstatsachen und Christliche Ethik' in *Diskussion zur 'politischen Theologie'*, Munich/Mainz, 1964, p. 238.
12 Cf. J. Moltmann, *Perspektiven der Theologie*, Munich/Mainz, 1968, pp. 174–188.
13 Cf. B. Häring, 'La novità della vita morale', in *Problemi attuali di teologia morale e pastorale*, Roma, 1967, 2nd ed. pp. 27–38.
14 Cf. Paul VI, *Evangelii nuntiandi*, n. 77; B. Häring, *Prospettive e problemi ecumenici di teologia morale*, Roma, 1973.
15 Cf. M. Cornelis, *Sortis du Ghetto: spiritualité de la pré-évangelisation à la lumière de Foucauld, Teilhard, Peyrguère*, Paris, 1964; A.-M. Nebreda, 'Pre-evangelizaciòn, primer estadio en al diàlogo de salvaciòn, in *Misiones Extranjeras* 15 (1968), pp. 1–15; W. Sacke, 'Pre-evangelizaciòn: justificaciòn teològica

vs condicionamentos etnològicos, in *Misiones Extranjeras* 15 (1968), pp. 33–58; A. Duval, 'La pré-évangelisation et le dialogue avec les non-chrétiens', in *Revue du Clergé Africain* 24 (1969), pp. 485–506; D. Grasso, 'Pre-evangelizzazione o evangelizzazione?' in *Rivista del Clero Italiano* 54 (1973), pp. 527–532.

16 Cf. B. Häring, *Faith and Morality in a Secular Age*, St Paul Publications, Slough, 1973, pp. 207–217.

17 Cf. H.R. Niebuhr, *Radical Monotheism and Western Culture*, New York, 1960.

2

The evangelization of morals

The morals of a person become evangelized and redeemed the moment the gospel is accepted, given the first place and lived according to its spirit. This is the point of encounter between the morals of evangelization and the evangelization of morals.

1. *The gospel encounters an already existing morality*

The good news is a call to conversion of the whole person in both personal and community dimensions. Abraham was not justified through the morals with which he entered the alliance, but through the alliance which offered new perspectives and presented further demands to his morals and to those of the Israelite people. The morals of the people, as all people, and the teaching of the priests would always need to be evangelized; in this consisted the principal task of the prophets. Christ gave to the morals of the Old Testament the fullness of the good news. He himself is *the Covenant* and *the Law*. With him the law dwells among men and through the Holy Spirit becomes the law of the new alliance inscribed in the heart. The golden rule, the centre of every noble morality, 'love your neighbour as yourself', acquires a new perspective and goes out vivified by the encounter with the gospel of the love of Christ: 'Love one another as I have loved you' (Jn 15 : 12). Morals are evangelized when people give themselves without reserve to the gospel and accept it as rule and norm of life. 'Be converted, and believe the gospel' (Mk 1 : 14).

It is obvious that the evangelization of morals assumes diverse stresses according to the system that is to be evangelized. The morals of the humble, of the *anawim*, receives without shock the happy message in Christ the Servant of God. The morals of the merciful, of the Samaritan, receives fullness from and is centred in the mercy of the Father who is revealed in

43

Christ the incarnate compassion. 'Be compassionate as your Father is compassionate.' (Lk 6 : 36).

Quite different is the encounter with the morals of the Pharisees, of the scribes and of the high priests. It is precisely their concept of morality and their 'justice according to the law' which must be overturned to give place to the gospel and its morality. To Paul it meant the harsh task of converting, evangelizing the morals of the Judeo-Christians, who with their erroneous absolutions and sacralizations, would have blocked not only the evangelization of the Gentiles, but also the development of a genuinely evangelical morals itself. A different task concerned him in regard to Stoic ethics, which was concordant with the gospel in its concept of wisdom, of self-perfection, of *ataraxia* (undisturbedness) and so on.

The Church finds herself today in front of a mission extremely difficult: to evangelize at the same time the morals of the secularized world, that of the great ethical religions of Asia, such as Confucianism and that of the spiritual religions such as Buddhism and Hinduism which, sensitive especially to contemplation, have not given to responsibility towards the world the place which belongs to it. Evangelization cannot be limited here to exporting a well made Christian-European morals: it is necessary to evangelize the morals already known and lived in the various cultures.

It is not, however, only pre-Christian morals that needs to be evangelized, but also the different forms which are developed and which have evolved from within the Church must be continuously deepened, purified and re-integrated through the gospel. There is always a danger that morals avoids the gospel and loses the sap of it, and this is true not only of morals as lived by the people or the clergy, but also of the morals of the moralists and their systems. The great evangelizers of morals are the saints: it is sufficient to think of St Francis who overturned and destroyed moralism with an insistent principle, 'We can, we must, and we want to live the gospel'.[1]

A classical text for the morals of evangelization and for the inverse process is the work of St Bernard, *De Consideratione ad Eugenium Tertium*.[2] In a very concrete and prophetically actual manner he affirms that the first task of the successor of Peter and of all the Church is evangelization, and therefore they should free themselves from the things which do not serve for this end. In this context the saint touched also upon the problem which is being treated here as it presented itself in the practice of his time, and he fought against intrusion of legalism. 'Everywhere noise and tumult . . . day by day they make a great din with laws, but those of Justinian, not of the Lord. . . . For the law of the Lord is pure converting the soul. But these are not so much laws as quarrels and quibbles, to overturn just judgement.'[3] Law and the use of morals have been falsified by motives which are not honest. 'From all over the world, the ambitious, the greedy, the simoniacs and all kinds of like monsters are gathering together either to get ecclesiastical honours from apostolic authority or to get them approved by it.'[4] The evangelization of morals denounces and unmasks ideologies. 'The Church is full of the striving of those who are ambitious for office. . . . She seems sometimes just a den of robbers who are looking for the goods of those who pass by'.[5] St Bernard clearly indicates the way to follow for the re-evangelization both of morals and of ecclesiastical law and the apostolic ministry: meditation on the gospel in view of the priority of preaching it. The first place should be given to meditation:[6] 'So that you may become a full integrated human being, may wisdom gather you too within the depths where all are received'.[7] The norm should be in all the 'the unlimited zeal of Paul and his free and generous charity.'[8]

2. 'It is the decision of the Holy Spirit, and our decision, to lay no further burden upon you beyond these essentials' (Acts 15 : 28).

The obligation to evangelize and to convert fully the different forms of morals that we meet today, confronts us with problems similar to those which confronted the Apostle of the Gentiles. First of all Paul had to desacralize and disabsolutize Hebrew morals, as received by the Judeo-Christian nomists. Without the charism and the fidelity of Paul Christianity would still remain a Judaic movement, a narrow sect for Jews and proselytes. Paul affirmed strongly the liberty of Christians in relation to the numerous norms coming from the Mosaic law and the explanation given it by various rabbinical schools. That which impelled and sustained him in the decisive way was the will to evangelize all nations, to whom the gospel would be able to display its charm when not hidden by a foreign morality, as in fact Judaic casuistry was.

But it was not a question of a wretched strategic problem: it was not the period of *marketing*. It was simply a problem of fidelity to the gospel.

Christ is not the servant of the Mosaic law, but Liberator and Saviour of all men. He came to destroy all man-made barriers, those also between Jews and Gentiles. What redeems us is grace and not morals, especially if our morals is not evangelical morals. Paul preaches, today as yesterday, a conversion to Christ and to his message of salvation, and not to a determined moral system.

In the evangelization of the Jews, Paul made himself a Jew, that is, he observed their customs and ethical norms, but at the same time he admonished the Judeo-Christians and Peter himself that it would be unjust to make their laws absolute and to want to impose them on people of other cultures and traditions. He therefore forced himself to evangelize his people, but did not forget that his charism imposed on him first of all to pay attention to the Gentiles. Christocentric and eschatological soteriology gave to Paul the courage and the liberty to reconstruct both the Hebraic morals and those of other cultures. The Acts of the Apostles and the letter to the Galatians indicate how long the fight which he had to sustain lasted. Many Judeo-Christians saw in Paul a kind of anarchical nihilist, an enemy of morality.[9] But in the end he obtained the support and the consent of the other apostles and the Church of Jerusalem (cf. Acts 15 : 1–35). Nevertheless he continued to encounter, till the end of his life, a vigorous opposition within the Church. Throughout the centuries, a similar resistance, to the detriment of evangelization and of the authenticity of the Christian life, has never been lacking.

Paul wanted to avoid even the least appearance that conversion to Christ signified in some way adherence to Judaism. Besides, he learnt, from his conversion and from the way in which Christ denounced the morals of the Pharisees, that the sacralization of a code of laws provokes the rise of false values because it tends to produce externalism, formalism, pride and hypocrisy. The apostle thought that the observance of the old law was a prerogative of infancy which preceded Christ's revelation, and that the spiritual adult, the Christian, had no need of such observances and relative control. 'As Christ had already first done, Paul wanted to eradicate the idea which considered religion as a code of laws with relative menaces of supernatural sanctions. True religion lives essentially in that love which fulfils voluntarily the law and which transcends by far all that which is demanded by the law.'[10]

For Paul, to be free from Judaic law means to be liberated by Christ for this perfect law, the law of oblative love which has its model in the love nourished by the Lord for us. The apostle is convinced that the law imposed from outside, especially when it is a matter of foreign customs, cannot liberate from egoism. On the other hand the believer finds in Christ himself his life and his law, which liberates us and makes us gladly fulfil the will of God: the law of justice, of love, of peace, of reconciliation.

There is always in Paul a preoccupation not to destroy valid customs proper to people to whom he brings the good news (cf. 1 Cor 11 : 1–16). One of the motives, even if not the only one, is evangelization, which cannot separate itself from the credibility of the Christian community. Christians must however discern and conserve all and only that which is just, good and honest (cf. 1 Thess 5 : 29). Paul contrasts with force Christian sanctity and bad pagan customs (cf. Eph 4 : 17–32). Every one of his moral exhortations finds its centre in the new life, the life in Christ — *einai en Xristô* (being in Christ) — an expression which occurs a hundred and sixty four times in his letters. The ultimate criterion for the moral life is not an external code, but the new reality of life in Christ and the mission confided to the people of God to witness to its salvation.

To the proud wisdom of the Greek philosophers Paul opposed the wisdom of the cross. But he does not limit himself to a polemic exposition of the new life in Christ; instead he looks for points through which to approach the morals and the ethical reflections of various people. Thus, for example, he referred frequently to the hellenistic concept of conscience (*syneidesis*), to demonstrate however at the end that it finds its true light and its dynamism in faith.[11]

The apostle accepted and stimulated dialogue even on the idea of the natural law,[12] but not in order to re-propose a system of ethical norms established by the philosophers or the Roman jurists, rather to affirm the presence of God, Creator and Redeemer, in the sincere conscience of man. 'When Gentiles who do not possess the law carry out its precepts by the light of nature, then, although they have no law, they are their own law, for they display the effects of the law inscribed in their hearts. Their conscience is called as witness, and their own thoughts argue the case on either side, against them or even for them' (Rom 2 : 14–15). Even here, he sees everything in the great perspective of redemptive love. There is no doubt that for him every morals, Judaic as well as Greek or Roman, stands in need of redemption: and this cannot take place if not through Jesus Christ and in the light of his gospel.

3. *The situation today in the light of Pauline theology*

The Church finds herself today at a crossroads similar to that in which she found herself at the time of Paul. She goes out, and must do so; she must leave the too narrow orbit of western culture and the western world, which were once considered simply as *the* world and *the* culture, but which are now old. Within a few decades the so-called *third world* — Asiatic, African and South American — will constitute more than three quarters of humanity and will have a young population, while the west becomes constantly older.

We must not however overlook the fact that even in this same western context the Church must free herself from a concept of culture and of cultural morals dominated by Greek, Roman and Germanic influences. The monopoly of Greco-Roman culture and of the precepts and natural laws which issued from it can no longer be sustained. The Church cannot avoid being aware that she finds herself faced with new generations for which the vision of the world is profoundly different from that in which ecclesiastical moral systems were formed.

Evangelization imposes on the Church the liberating duty of abandoning a clerical, juridical and centralistic concept of her government, modelled on and deeply marked by the out-dated political systems of the western world. The time of colonialism which so much influenced the idea of mission, of evangelization and finally of morals is now past. Discussing neo-colonialism we become aware of the ethico-juridical neo-colonialism of which the Church would be guilty if she would want to continue to impose centralistic and diplomatic methods, in moral pedagogy and in the uniformity of canon law with exasperating relative controls; these things could never be completely inspired by the gospel, though they were to a great extent acceptable in past epochs. Now on the contrary there would not be any justification however small: the Church must be conscious of the inter-dependence of her juridico-administrative system with a past system and a political praxis which inevitably provoke alienation and contestation today.

The Church is coming out of an epoch which sees her as having the characteristics or 'the Church and the Empire' or 'the Church of the state'. Her government and her juridico-moral schemes were profoundly marked by the privileged situation of the clergy and, above all, the hierarchy. The entire action of the government of the Church and the application and control of moral and juridical principles (often confused and mixed up) were conditioned by that situation, of which the most humiliating expression in the concrete was the principle in vogue at the epoch of the Reformation *cuius regio eius et religio.* Here the hierarchicalChurch played a political role which was quite weighty; but, the Christian princes — Catholics as well as Protestants — reserved to themselves the right to determine the religion of their subjects. Actually the process of secularization is practically at its end in the lay world, while in the Church many structures and systems corresponding to the past situation are still conserved.[13]

If we were aware of the new dimensions in which man and the world which must be evangelized are to be found we could no longer sustain a desire to be concerned only with the diverse casuistic applications of established moral principles.[14] The Church's essential mission, to evangelize not only individuals but the world — nations, cultures and their moral approaches — imposes on her the obligation to understand fully the new situation, and this demands profound fidelity to the gospel and courageous use of her successes and failures in evangelization, humbly remembered, from her past experience — the failures often caused by lack of awareness of the diversity of cultures and their moralities.

4. *A continuous and universal task*

The evangelization of morals and various systems of morals is a continuous process as is that of the individual conversion of each person and the renewal of the Church and society. We shall never arrive at a point where we could consider ourselves fully satisfied by the perspective, the dynamism and the evangelical content of a particular system, a particular type of theology or moral pedagogy. And it is not even possible to perpetuate mechanically the major successes which have in certain circumstances been achieved in this sphere. In fact, all that which is not rethought, is not interiorized and does not insert itself in a fresh dialogue, inevitably ossifies itself within new conditions. It would be still worse if we wanted simply to reduce ourselves to conserving and repeating those moral models which, from the beginning, have been a partial failure or an extremely limited success in relation to the evangelization of morals.

The incarnation of the moral message of the gospel in cultures, experiences and new generations demands the capacity to 'disincarnate' itself, that is, to separate itself, from successive pasts and to renounce firmly any indolence or intellectual and spiritual inertia.

Evangelization of morals and of the diverse systems of morals is, as I have already said, something completely different from a simple casuistic application of the old norms to new cases presented by recent cultures. Rather, it is a question of a new fermentation of the morality lived and, also, of the great current theories, of a dialogue with the spirit of the epoch.[15]

As Christ has confided to his Church the mission to proclaim the gospel to every nation, transforming the morals of all cultures and generations, it is inevitable that there will be a pluralism not only in the field of scientific theology, which always serves for a certain historical moment or for a particular culture,[16] but, and still much more, in that of moral pedagogy, however nearer to the diversity of life. Since the one Church does not only permit but claims a pluralism of local churches, to make visible that her unity is founded on the presence of the Holy Spirit and to manifest the faith in Christ Emmanuel, God with all, the necessity of a sound pluralism of theology and particularly of moral theologies is undeniable, always however under that impulsion of the effort for an authentic evangelization of morals.[17] *The International Theological Commission* appointed by Paul VI prepared an important document entitled *Faith and theological pluralism*. This document touches also on the moral problem. 'Pluralism in the moral field appears above all to be in the application of general principles to concrete circumstances. This becomes yet more extensive when contacts are established with cultures which at the beginning were ignored, or on account of rapid changes in society. All the same a fundamental unity is manifested through the common esteem of human dignity, which implies imperatives for the conduct of life. The conscience of every man expresses a certain number of fundamental exigencies recognized in our age in public declarations on the essential rights of man. The unity of Christian morals is founded on constant principles, contained in the scriptures, presented to each generation by the magisterium. Let us remember the principal lines of force: the teachings and example of the Son of God who revealed the heart of the Father, the disposition of his death and resurrection, the life according to the Spirit in the bosom of his Church, in faith, in hope and in charity to renew us according to the image of God. The necessary unity of faith and communion does not impede a diversity of vocations and personal preferences in the manner of approaching the mystery of Christ and of living it.'[18]

The affirmed unity as well as the pluralism in the field of morals will acquire great strength if everything is seen and confronted in the perspective of the evangelization of every nation, culture, generation and social class. The encounter of faith with the morality lived and with the concrete system of the moral values incarnate in a certain culture remains always decisive. For example, while the scale of values of the Roman culture or of the Greek *polis* required morals which gave preference to prudence, with a political shading, the great cultures and religions of Asia will necessitate an absolute precedence for the aspects of benevolence and gentleness. The gospel enters normally through the gate of the value which appeals more or which occupies the first place in the scale. When the principal value is effectively evangelized, deepened or enriched with new dimensions, it will be relatively easy to evangelize the entire morals of the culture which includes it.

5. *Some models of the evangelization of morals*

The discussion of the necessity of the christianization, or evangelization, of every historical form of morals would remain vague if it were not exemplified from past experience.[19] This gives us a real pluralism of moral approach within the Church as a result of the endeavour to evangelize the various pre-existing systems.

A. *An imperative moral system*

The gospel, like the Old Testament revelation before it, meets often a system of an exterior moral imperative bound to a precise control of the observance of traditional norms. The more remote parts of the Old Testament contain an apodictic morals. The traditions and the imperatives of the great tribal heads of Israel became a divine commandment and indispensable demand of the gratuitous alliance; the observance is concretized as solidarity with the people and a glorifying of the God of the alliance. But from the beginning evangelization has a place in the process of interiorization which is above all the work of the great prophets.[20] Full evangelization is accomplished in Christ, who began by contrasting dynamic laws with purely prohibitive laws: 'You have learned that our forefathers were told. . . . But what I tell you is this. . .' (Mt 5).

More or less successful or unsuccessful attempts at evangelizing morals based on laws and imperatives are found in the whole history of the Church. She sought to give an evangelical breath to the natural laws and to the natural and civil rights originally thought out by the philosophers or Roman judges. In the epoch of paternalism, and princely absolutism, scientific morals and in yet a greater measure pedagogical morals presented themselves as motivations of such laws, still establishing them, at least partially, and surmounting them. The classical manuals of the Roman type show, from the eighteenth century onwards, an effort in this sense; it did not always succeed, and this because there was no kerygmatic approach, but rather one limited to the ends of ecclesiastical control.

B. *The evangelization of philosophies of natural law*

It is true there were many attempts aimed at giving an evangelical dimension to different ethical philosophies of natural law, but rarely did they succeed in showing the relation between the law of Christ and these ethics. In consideration of the importance assumed by the basic rights of every man and people, indicated and declared by the United Nations Organization, we find ourselves faced now with a necessary endeavour to understand and illustrate the place which belongs to such rights in an evangelical vision of personal and social life.[21]

C. *The morals of obedience and of loyalty*

An imperative moral system has various points of contact with a morality which puts obedience and fidelity first. I am thinking especially of the influence exercised by the Germanic tribes for whom the supreme value was absolute loyalty to the princes. In this context evangelization was carried out as a transfer: the only person who merits loyalty and absolute following is Christ. On account of the predominant role frequently played by the Christian princes either in the conversion of their tribes or in their relation with the ecclesiastical authorities, an obedience practically blind and total to the state and ecclesiastical laws was accepted and sustained with excessive ease. The attempt to integrate such a type of ethics with Christian faith rarely escapes the danger of the arrogance of the powerful and the immaturity and moral underdevelopment of the masses. Historically it did not pay attention to the virtue of discernment and to prophetic *parrhesia* (boldness). The temptation was particularly great where this moral philosophy presented itself as the only Christian and Catholic moral philosophy.

D. *The morals of autoperfection*

Already in the first centuries a great effort was made on the part of theology and pastoral theory to evangelize the morals of autoperfection existing then. Practically all the moral systems of the Hellenistic world — especially the Stoic, the Aristotelean and the Platonic — were of this sort: in the centre was man, even if not as such, but in so far as he was free and masculine, desirous of self-realization. The virtues were ways in which this self-perfection was manifested and realized. This, at least, was the dominant perspective. On the one hand, Christianity, with its message of the eternal Word made man for our salvation, could comfortably approach this anthropocentric ethics.[22] On the other hand, however, such egoistic anthropocentrism could not fail to be vigorously contested by the law of grace and of justice coming from God, who obliges us not only to our own self-realization but to the acceptance and service of his kingdom and of our neighbour. The rebirth of humanism adopted ethical eudemonism, a moral doctrine having as a principle that the end of an action is happiness, (from the Greek *eudaimoneo*, to be happy), without ever overcoming clearly an anthropocentrism closed in itself and the temptation to Pelagianism. This did not fail to influence also the morals and the pedagogy of the Church.

The four cardinal virtues — prudence, justice, fortitude and temperance — became, alongside the three theological virtues — faith, hope and charity — the canon of the virtues. This systematization certainly did not derive from the gospel, which rather puts in focus the eschatological virtues — thanksgiving, hope, and vigilance, and the detachment-openness and mortification-joy pairs. In view of evangelization, however, the fathers of the Church assumed the prevalently Greek system of the cardinal virtues. St Augustine, in particular, made great efforts to give them a typically Christian perspective and motivation. 'As far as the virtues which lead to the beatific life are concerned, I say that they do not exist if not as the summary of charity towards God. As I see it, the fourfold structure of virtue is linked to an articulation of love — not, however, any kind of love, but love for God, the supreme Good, supreme Wisdom and Unity. It is therefore possible to make the essential definition already given more precise: temperance is love which preserves itself intact and unviolated for God; fortitude is love which bears everything easily for God; justice is love which serves God exclusively and, therefore, leads to a right order all that is subject to man; prudence is love which knows how to distinguish what can be useful to it from what can be an obstacle on the way to God'.[23]

When however this western schema would claim to teach the east we find ourselves before an ossification, before an ethical colonialism and before a most typical unsuccessful evangelization. The four books of Confucius express oriental cultural heritages and are much nearer to the gospel than is the Stoic system. 'The greatest gift which heaven has given to the wise are the virtues of benevolence, gentleness, justice and prudence. They have their roots in the heart. Their effects radiate from the face.'[24] The Confucian doctrine offers above all the advantage of a perspective similar to that of the gospel; besides seeing in all the gift of heaven it has at its centre benevolence and a man's rightness of heart in relation to his neighbour.

E. *The morals of order*

In the Roman Empire the concept of *ordo hierarchicus*, the established order, was united to the notion of the *Pax Romana*. Evangelization could not ignore a value so dear to that culture. St Augustine made a precious contribution with his concept of *ordo amoris*. The first place, therefore, must not be occupied by the established order of the Empire, but by the one which issues from faith and a renewed heart. In the theology of St Thomas also the idea had a privileged place which reflected the demands of the contemporary culture and society. Thus the morals of order could bring about an integration of the value of custom and the social order, which remained always one of the founts of ethics, and of the dynamics of love.[25] This did not prevent the morals of order from often losing its identity and its evangelical fervour, especially when it came to serve a static vision of the world and of order. This is what happened particularly at the time of political and ecclesiastical restoration.

F. *The sacramental perspective of Christian morals*

Christ has evangelized and transformed the most fundamental human experiences through a sacramental vision. He himself is in the centre, the great Sacrament which renders visible the love of the Father. Already the morals of St John and St Paul are primarily sacramental morals. This model has prevailed in the oriental Orthodox Churches up to today.[26] It will however be remembered that here it is not a question of a technical concept of sacrament, as it appeared in the Latin manuals of the last centuries. In the eyes of the Orthodox Churches of the great oriental tradition even the created universe, historical events and every human experience, become sacraments, because for the believer they become visible signs of the love, patience, greatness, grace and forgiveness of God and, together, the response of man rendered possible by divine grace. Therefore, in the final analysis, it is a question of a meeting with the more decisive human experiences, seen however in the light of Christ, the great Sacrament, the 'visible Image of the invisible God'. This approach is always valid, but it presupposes a very deep experience of the sacraments, and of the sacramentality of the Church in relationship to the whole of human life, and furthermore, a certain sensitivity to the signs and fundamental acts in which the heart of the believer and the qualities of the community are expressed. A sacramental vision of this kind could encounter other ethical systems as an evangelizing stimulus and form a unique synthesis with them. It demands an on-going generous effort of renewal of the whole life and the structures of the Church.

G. *The morals of responsibility*

The most important values in the actual secular world are those of responsibility, liberty, sincere conscience, solidarity, maturity and discernment. All these values have their meeting point in the morals of responsibility, to which every valuable section of today's society adheres. Jewish and Christian theologians have contributed very much to placing these values in the light of revelation: God speaks to us and gives us the capacity to respond; he unites us in the alliance so that we can give a solidary response. The works of F. Ebner, M. Buber, R. Guardini, T. Steinbüchel, G. Marcel, E. Mounier, K. Barth, and especially D. Bonhoeffer, R. Niebuhr and J. M. Gustafson follow the approach,[27] leading to a Christianity to which we belong by vocation and free choice, which will take the place of the Christianity of the state or the empire. This cannot, however, be the unique moral model to be proposed to every culture and generation of the world. Nevertheless, to me it is one of the unrelinquishable perspectives, because I think that the whole of humanity is on the path of development towards a culture which, notwithstanding diversities and tensions, generally shows great sensibility in the confrontations of such values. The evangelization of the secular morals of responsibility is one of the essential aspects in the very wide context of the total evangelization of morals.

This evangelization must take due care especially of the principle of the autonomy of the various temporal spheres as it is affirmed in article thirty six of *Gaudium et spes.*[28]

6. *The dimensions and limits of the evangelization of morals*

The process of christianization and re-christianization of morals, customs and the whole of morality implies always a great complexity, of which the mystery of sin is an inevitable part. The problem becomes more acute in relation to the affirmation of an autonomous morals and of a tendency, also within the Church, which aims at sustaining the value of human reason, while giving little attention to the light of Christ and the darkness of sin. As we must be very careful in speaking of '*faith and works*', so must we also avoid a too simplistic vision of '*faith and reason*' or, worse still, of '*reason and faith*'. We may ask ourselves of what reason it is a question. Is it a question of the redeemed reason which voluntarily subordinates itself to the light of faith or of the reason which pretends to place itself beside, if not directly above, faith? Works, however great, are worth nothing on the plane of salvation and evangelization if they do not issue from faith and grace and if they are not united in the witness of faith. Besides, where religion is subordinated to other spheres, reason becomes the greater antagonist of faith; whereas if the Gospel and faith occupy the first place reason is of great service to them.[29] This truth must never be lost sight of if the following pages are to be correctly evaluated.

The evangelization of the world and of morals — both the morals foreign to the Church and the morals of Christians 'baptized' but never completely permeated by the vision of the gospel — is always a duty of the whole Church, but a particular role is confided to the magisterium. The effectiveness and purity of the hierarchical and sacerdotal ministry depend on faith, on witnessing and on the co-responsibility of all the faithful.[30] The evangelization of morals in the concrete and in various cultural and social conditionings belongs above all to the local Churches. But to overcome egoistic particularism, the effort of the universal Church and its central government, aiming to avoid a non-authentic pluralism which is in contradiction to the essential unity and the dynamism of faith, is very necessary indeed. It is above all a matter of promoting genuine dialogue.

It is worth repeating that it is not a question of creating a morals *ex nihilo*, but of evangelizing that which is already existing and which manifests the work of God and, at the same time, the marks of sin and of individual and collective alienation.

A. *The recognition of all that is valid*

In the first place we must in a Eucharistic spirit say that it is just and dutiful to recognize the good existing in the customs, the most cherished values and the common reflections of a particular culture, social class or new generation; in fact, it is through these things that the presence of God, Creator and Redeemer, operates. 'Whatever is true, whatever is honourable, whatever is just, whatever is pure, whatever is lovely, whatever is gracious, if there is any excellence, if there is anything worthy of praise, think about these things' (Phil 4 : 8). In this passage of St Paul his preoccupation to refer to the mystery of Christ all that is valid in the morals that are to be evangelized is evident.

B. *The critical prophetic role*

To recognize and accept all that is good, true and beautiful demands discernment, possible through the light of the gospel in the co-reflection which is listening and prayer. As morals and concrete moral systems are composed of various elements mixed together, in which unfortunately there are seeds of discord spread by the enemy, the Church, that is, the entire people of God and particularly the pastors and the prophets, must denounce courageously, with *parrhesia* (boldness), both egoism and collective and individual prejudices. It is a question of desacralizing the 'sacred egoism' which so many taboos have created in various religions and ethical systems, and which has sometimes fraudulently introduced itself, as a Trojan horse, into certain parts of ecclesiastical morals which are encouraged by clerical privilege and the alienation of ecclesiastics from the common and social life.[31]

It is especially necessary to interrogate prophetically those moral systems which demand freedom not only from domination by the clergy (which is just), but also from confrontation with the gospel and with the humble proclamation which the Church makes of it. She must always be firm in the denunciation of moral disorders, but must multiply her energies when these dare hypocritically to present themselves as progress, liberty, independence, and so on.[32] To be listened to, however, the voice of the Church must be free from all desire of domination, while at the same time courageous in denouncing not only the sins of the humble and the oppressed but especially the prejudices and the failures of the privileged, oppressing, powerful, or organized classes of society. The prophetic voice of the Church is genuine when she does not allow herself to be instrumentalized or manipulated by the powerful of whatever sort they may be. Most especially, those who feel themselves educated, and so despise 'the little people', need to be interrogated very critically.[33] The self-sufficiency of those who do not want to serve and, consequently, who do not adore the one God, needs to be put under prophetic judgement.

C. *The integrating role*

All that is valid or that can at least become valid should be integrated into the dynamic vision of faith. The re-integration of morals — the fruit of the shared experiences and reflections of diverse cultures, social classes and generations — reaches an acceptable point of maturation only when everything enters into the light of Christ and the particular norms become blended together and insert themselves into the great dynamism of the law of faith, grace and love, as it is marvellously expressed in the Sermon on the Mount and, with special intensity, in the beatitudes and in the seven dynamic affirmations, 'But I say to you. . .' (Mt 5).

D. *Openness to new dimensions and demands*

When re-integration and prophetic discernment progress, new dimensions and new demands which had remained hidden to the wise and to every form of morals not yet evangelized are opened up and understood. Here I should like to remember and re-think all that was said in the first part about the *signs of the times*, the *kairos*, and the conditions which permit them to be perceived and recognized. The imperatives which arise in view of such demands and opportunities, overwhelm and transcend the possibilities of autonomous reason, that is, reason not enlightened by faith, but will never place themselves in contradiction to the more authentic experience and the more sincere shared reflections of all men and women of good will.

Of great importance is the law of growth: the progress of the re-integration of morals can advance only with the growth of a living faith in persons and communities, and also only in this growth of a living faith in persons and communities can new dimensions and new evangelical demands be laid open.

E. *The sacred ethos and the sanctioned ethos*

Rudolf Otto with his comparative study of major religions has rendered a great service to the elucidation of the relation between faith and morals.[34] Where the sacred *ethos* is not mature because not meeting with an infinitely holy merciful God, it does not, as it should, exercise on customs any critical and purifying influence, while it tends unfortunately to offer them with excessive facility a sanction of a religious character.

Thus we see that in many religions and, in some epochs, even in Christianity, a religiousness not sufficiently deepened or enlightened has sanctioned things which the living faith would have without doubt eliminated. An example in this regard is provided by the Pharisees, who empowered human traditions with sacralizing sanctions to the detriment of demands more true to the faith. In the history of the Church afterwards, it is sufficient to point to sacred sanctions in favour of clerical domination, torture, so-called 'sacred wars' and religious fanaticism, which was often an obstacle to a sincere search for the will of God.

In every religion we find an interpenetration of sacred *ethos* and sanctioned *ethos*. Religious man always feels that there is a relation between the transcendental world and daily reality; but, the mode of defining this relation is often conditioned by a kind of religious short-circuit. Secularization can be transformed into grace or, at least, into a challenge, obliging all religions, especially Christianity, to present the relation between faith and morals in a more convincing, more dynamic and clearer way. The more humbly believers and the entire Church recognize the limits of their competence and the necessity to progress simultaneously in the knowledge of God, of man and his world, the more authentic will be the sanctions and the dynamism which faith offers to the proper moral exigencies of life.[35] Nevertheless it seems to me erroneous to attribute to the sacred *ethos*, even in its most perfect form, in the Christian faith, the exclusive role of sanctioning the *ethos* already existing and the moral norms previously deduced by reason. I consider essential, for one who explicitly knows Christ and the new life in him and lives in the community of faith and praise of God, the discovery of moral exigencies which derive directly from the revelation made to us in Christ or manifested as a cry of creatures who aspire to participation in the liberty of the children of God (cf. Rom 8 : 20-23).

7. *The evangelization of canon law*[36]

The fundamental law of the Church is always the gospel;

it is the gospel that will instruct us in the law of the Spirit which renews the heart of man and the face of the earth. The gospel is in a unique sense the *jus sacrum*. Nevertheless the Church needs also juridical institutions and structures which can correspond to the demands of various cultures and societies.[37] What has been said to be valid for morals, that is, that it is always in need of evangelization, applies more, and more specifically, to canon law. The Church can never limit herself simply to adopting the *jus profanum*, even the *jus Romanum*, and this because of her specific nature and mission. However, there will always be a tendency in canon law, and especially in those who administer it, to forget or ignore the evangelical vision and spirit.

The Second Vatican Council, after having underlined the necessity of perfecting moral theology in such a way that 'its scientific exposition should be more thoroughly nourished by scriptural teaching, should show the nobility of the Christian vocation of the faithful, and their obligation to bring forth fruit in charity for the life of the world', has a demanding and inspiring word for canon law: 'in the explanation of canon law the mystery of the Church should be kept in mind, as it was set forth in the dogmatic constitution on the Church promulgated by this Holy Synod' (*Optatam totius*, 16). Paul VI applied this text in depth underlining that it is necessary 'to derive the canonical law from the essence itself of the Church of God, through which the new and original law, which is evangelical, is love, is the "grace of the Holy Spirit given by faith in Christ" (*Summa Theologica*, 1–2 : 106 : 1 : c). Thus if this is the interior principle which guides the Church in her work it should always be manifest in her visible, exterior and social discipline. It is easier to insist on this vision than to forsee all the consequences'[38]

To counteract the insidious anti-institutional tendencies which explicitly or practically deny the Church the *jus divinum* to issue laws, I shall try to propose some principles on the use of law in the Church.

A. — All the disciplinary and normative complexus of the Church finds its authentic value in the evangelical service of salvation in Christ. Law and its administration must be radically subordinated to the mission of the Church to bring the gospel to all nations. The gospel is the unique and true constitutional charter of the Church. Every other valid norm tends only to indicate the ways along which it is possible to announce and live its riches, incarnating it in time and space, to develop thus the seed of the kingdom of God which forms the entire riches of the Church.

B. — In all her life the Church has as her inner norm the grace of the Spirit who 'guides the Church into all truth and unites her in communion and service. He provides and directs her with various gifts, both hierarchical and charismatic, and adorns her with his fruits. By the power of the gospel he makes the Church young again, perpetually renews her, and leads her to perfect union with her Bridegroom' (*Lumen gentium*, 4).

Animated by the Spirit, the Church accepts with gratitude the gift of the revelation of the Father in Christ and in him we respond with the obedience of faith which directs and purifies every form of obedience. The Church's response of faith follows the rhythm of the liturgy, especially of the Eucharistic celebration, and makes her gradually discover all the exigencies of faith and the true life according to the law of grace.

The Spirit guides the Church enriching her as he likes and when he likes with his gifts, both ministries and charisms. All these are at the service of the growth of the entire Body of Christ. Canonical legislation should never and in no way be an instrument of an authority which dominates but of a *diakonia*, through which the Spirit makes the Church grow in fidelity to the gospel and in saving service to all humanity.

C. — The discipline of the Church, both in its contents and in its language, should reflect in the first place not a 'society' juridically articulated in terms of authority and its subjects, of rights and duties, but the riches, the profundity and the immensity of the mystery of Christ, 'who loved the Church as his Bride, delivering himself up for her in order to sanctify her. He united her to himself as his own body and crowned her with the gift of the Holy Spirit to the glory of God' (*Lumen gentium*, 39). Canonical legislation is not a service to the *status quo* but one that gives stability to the pilgrim Church on her journey towards the *parousia*. All this legislation should be a way of the living faith which stirs up hope and vigilance and works through charity. It is a way along which must be realized the unique sanctity of those who 'are moved by the Spirit of God, and who, obeying the voice of the Father, worshipping God the Father in spirit and in truth, follow the poor and humble Christ, bearing his cross, in order to be made worthy of sharing in his glory' (*Lumen gentium*, 41).

Because she is first of all a *koinonia* (fellowship, communion) in the Spirit, the Church transcends, in her legislation, the laws of earthly societies. Both the action of those who formulate ecclesial discipline and the action of those who carry it out should be inspired by the word of the Lord: 'The Sabbath was made for man, not man for the Sabbath' (Mk 2 : 27). Every norm should be formulated and carried out as a service to the dignity of the vocation and communion of the children of God in Christ. This is easier said than done.

D. — The legislation of the Church should always be an expression of her watchfulness for the *signs of the times* and should therefore exclude any ossification and any generalization which could contradict the real opportunities of the present. The pilgrim Church examines constantly the signs of the times in order to grasp opportunities and to respond to the necessities of various epochs and cultures, not only in the formulating but also in the carrying out of the law. Canonical legislation is evangelized in as much as it is a fruit of this watchfulness for the signs of the times and a constructive answer to them, a stimulus to the entire Church in her obligation to be at the service of the true necessities of humanity, and a source of precautionary measures for all her members and local communities in relation to dangers arising for the faith in certain circumstances of its existence at a particular moment.

E. — 'The human race has passed from a more static concept of reality to a more dynamic, evolutionary one' (*Gaudium et spes*, 5). Still more dynamic is the *journey* of the Church, since she is journeying towards 'her full perfection when the time of the restoration of all things will come. Then the human race as well as the whole world, which is intimately related to man and achieves its purpose through him, will be perfectly re-established in Christ' (*Lumen gentium*, 48).

The discipline of the Church is at the service of this dynamism of growth and of expectation: it is the discipline of a living community on the march. It should therefore be characterized by flexibility and by the call to vigilance in order to understand new opportunities and single out new dangers to which man is exposed in a concrete historical situation. Such a dynamic vision, especially in the present situation, should reveal itself also in an attitude of the universal Church towards encouraging the responsible initiatives of the local Churches. It should create a climate of confidence and co-responsibility, explaining the criteria of discernment to uphold, in a context of co-responsibility for the whole Church and for the vitality of the single Churches.

Only in those cases, well determined by the law, in which its necessity for the common good of the local Churches and of the future of the Church is evident, should the initiative be left to the central government and legislation.

F. — In the *diakonia* of the pastors, 'the Lord Jesus Christ is present in the midst of the faithful' (*Lumen gentium*, 21). He is particularly present in the *diakonia* of the successor of St Peter, who is called to confirm his brethren in faith and humility and thus to continue the pastoral mission of Christ. To the pope, therefore, and to the other pastors is due love, homage and co-operation in a spirit of co-responsibility, of sincerity and of frankness. The categories 'power', 'might', 'authority', 'right to obedience' should be lived, in the Church, according to the words and example of Christ who came to serve and not to be served (cf. Mt 20 : 28). The pastors and ministers of the Church are called to be witnesses to the gospel of the Servant Messiah and to the Church who is a handmaid, at the service of a people to whom is directed the call to maturity according to the measure of Christ.

The universal legislation of the Church is particularly a fruit of the service which the successors of Peter in collegiality with the bishops are invited to render to the unity in love of the community: it should be accepted with humility and 'Christian obedience' (*Lumen gentium*, 37). 'For those ministers who are endowed with sacred power are servants of their brethren, so that all who are of the people of God, and therefore enjoy a true Christian dignity, working together to the same end, freely and in an orderly way, can arrive at salvation' (*Lumen gentium*, 18). Ecclesial legislation should not aim to create barriers within the Church and between her and the world, but to make the life of all members of the people of God reflect the mystery of the Word incarnate and of his Church which is at the generous service of all humanity.

Therefore, the formulation, the explanation and the application of juridical norms, should take into account the responsibility and co-operation of all members of the Church who have a particular competence and a deep knowledge of the actual conditions of life and of the possible development of new forms of life.

G. — The life of the Church will be characterized by a sober use of positive laws: in this she testifies that she puts her confidence in the power of the Spirit. The pastors, who are such by the unction of the same Spirit, should be the example in this to their brethren.

However, as long as the earthly pilgrimage lasts, pastoral directives and the necessary disciplinary norms which sustain unity and charity, should never be lacking.

Pastors should however lay shares on the priority of prayer, confidence in grace, witnessing, patient exhortation and loving fraternal correction even in those cases in which, for the sake of moral improvement and for the protection of the basic rights of all, they have recourse to laws or sanctions.

H. — In the course of her history, the Church has expressed her original structure, articulated in various ministries through the will of Christ, incarnating it in the socio-cultural context to which she was sent to announce the gospel. For fidelity to her mission entrusted to her by Christ and for an effective functioning of her ministries, a continuous and courageous involvement is necessary, through discernment of what is essential from what is mutable, and through incarnation in what humanity gradually discovers and realizes as valuable and relevant.

I. — Every single point and every single formulation of ecclesial legislation should always be examined in the light of the Lord's will, 'that all may be one'. This is a fundamental criterion for the authenticity of all the life of the Church and it imposes a continuous and rigorous self-examination. If this criterion demands flexibility from legislation, it also demands on the part of all members of the Church a keen sense of the limits within which criticism should be exercised. If this would threaten unity and provoke scandal or disorientation, it would no longer be a prophetic service and authentic *parrhesia*, but a laceration of the Church.

J. — All the people of God, particularly its pastors, should receive with gratitude the prophetic voices of the saints whom the Spirit unceasingly raises up. Pastors have an eminent duty in the discernment of charisms, and especially of prophetic voices. In the fulfilment of this duty they can never however leave out dialogue and co-operation, ever broader and more open, between all the members of the Church.

K. — When pastors present a reform of ecclesiastical legislation to their brethren, that spirit of respect which flows from the dignity of the children of God co-responsible for the unity and the growth of all the brethren should be remembered. This spirit of respect excludes, on the one hand, the haughty disobedience of hearts closed to charity and, on the other hand, every form of servile or degrading obedience.

The Church is grateful to her Lord for all the good which, in the past, was derived from canonical discipline. However, she also confesses the sins committed and the defects brought about in the name of this same discipline. Accepting with gratitude and humility her own past, she asks how to explain and apply canonical discipline so as to draw benefit from the experience of the past and to accept in every form a service of charity and a stimulus to common research, in a humble and courageous co-operation, which values all competence and all the charisms and gifts of God.

In the application of the law one should never forget the fundamental principle of *aequitas canonica* which can be deepened through the theological traditions of *epikeia* and of the eastern *oikonomia*. In this way it becomes clear that canon law will be read and applied not according to the letter which kills, but according to the spirit which gives life.

8. *A difficult transition without ruptures*

The task of the evangelization of this pluralistic and immensely dynamic world, especially of morals and the law, is very arduous and only confidence in grace allows us to confront it with equilibrium. There has been a delay in renewal and in our awareness of the world in which we live. Hence arises a danger from the temptation to be hasty in transformations, which would inevitably fall into superficiality and into disorder. A great many Christians are intellectually and spiritually little prepared to confront the difficulties and opportunities of the present hour. It is a question of exodus, not less courageous and painful than those which were asked of Abraham and Moses.[39] The permanent council of the French Episcopate, in a document entitled *From a morality of laws to a morality of liberty*, indicates both the difficulties and the opportunities inherent in the renewal of morals: "Morals is above all faith lived and incarnated in the life of man. It expresses the demands of the evangelical ideal and of the testimony which every Christian has to give in his daily life. . . conscious of the differences of time this renewal must aim largely at opening our moral teaching to a positive comprehension of human realities, restoring to it a character more purely evangelical, in such a way that it can avoid the double accusation of dehumanization and naturalism.'[40]

This great task must be carried forward with courage and with the firm intention of overcoming its risks. To reject or to ignore the signs of the times would be a very major risk. And in the case where changes disregard and hurt the rearguard, we must not forget that the Church of the exodus has to be equally concerned about both rear-guards and vanguards. She must love the first just as much as the second. The sociologists and social-psychologists have said clearly that the future will be constituted by a dynamic two or three per cent of persons or groups. The Church must not abandon or lose those without whom she would not have, in human terms, any future in the world of tomorrow.[41] It would be an error to destroy elements of popular Christianity or of the mass in favour of a Church which appeals to the forward-looking spirit of the age if such a destruction would prevent us from effectively evangelizing Christians defined as 'ritualists' or 'traditionalists', but the mistake would not be smaller to conserve these elements without adding there a continuous effort to educate all to a more mature faith.[42]

As a first step it is a question of instructing all, so that they will understand the situation of the Church and the motives for which changes are imposed. Above all we must be very conscious that substantially it is a question of a more total adherence to the gospel and of a more interior and convinced fidelity to the Lord of history.

We must make a clear distinction between the vanguards, between that of the 'progressives', who have the courage to translate the gospel into practice, and that of the 'liberals', who are looking rather for an all too easy adaptation to the world. And if we must counsel the rear-guard (the conservatives) to understand better the meaning of the history of salvation and to live the exodus and continuous conversion, we must equally induce the progressives to show discretion in their confrontations with the so-called traditionalists, who are often humble people of good will and who are easily confused. We should follow the example of St Paul, the apostle of liberty, who voluntarily refused the right to support himself through serving the gospel (cf. 1 Cor 9 : 15ff) and taught the strong ones of the Church of Corinth not to give themselves to an abstract progressivism but to advance in charity and liberty which takes into consideration the conscience of the weak (cf. 1 Cor 8 : 1–15; Rom 14 : 1–15 : 3).

Patience and a respect for the real possibilities of growth which the Church must now show in the continuous process of the evangelization of the world and of morals, should never be misunderstood as a renunciation of the full ideal and of the evangelical norm.

The renewal linked with the evangelization of the world, of society, of morals and of law, is not possible without full acceptance of the inevitable situations of conflict. But, above all the conflict and the reciprocal criticism must reign faith in the reconciliation of Christ, the readiness for dialogue and the will to respect those who think differently, and who therefore, walk towards the future in a different rhythm. In this complex situation the law of Christ which asks all to carry one another's burdens stands in the centre (cf. Gal. 6 : 2). In a pastoral letter published in preparation for the Holy Year of 1975 the German bishops wrote, 'It is not sufficient to accept the necessity of living in conflict; it is also necessary to be committed to overcoming the conflicts.'

Any kind of psychological, psychosocial or disciplinary repression is surely not the way to overcome conflict, as this would sooner or later lead to explosive and destructive eruption. The way is that of Christ the Prophet, speaking truth boldly and in charity. Mahatma Gandhi has practised in a most exemplary way the evangelical virtue of nonviolence: on the one hand *Satyágraha*: an indefatigable, solitary search for more light, unmasking idols and ideologies, misuse of religion for the sake of power and wealth; on the other hand *Ahimsa*: sympathy for those who think and act differently and with whom confrontation in the search for greater purity and light is unavoidable.

The wounds that hurt the poor and block genuine evangelization have to be called by their real name, but it has to be done with the healing love of Christ.

*　　*　　*

This chapter was written in 1973. Everyone who is fully aware of polarizations in the Church today will see that they are, at present, of even more burning relevance. Men trained in old-fashioned canon law and well placed within the present wave of fundamentalism, try to impose the thought patterns of canon law of the Constantinian era, of centralism and harsh systems of control on moral theology, at least in all matters concerning sexuality. Representatives of the restorative, centralisitic trend openly question the applicability of the social principle of subsidiarity, so emphatically taught by the magisterium as a basic principle of all social life, or suggest that it should not be applied before the question of applicability to Church structures is fully studied. Thus they try to make for themselves a quiet conscience while blocking genuine structural renewal and the removal of sinful structures.

Everyone who has influence in the Church has to reflect most earnestly on the meaning and implication of the call for a new evangelization in view of the third millennium.

NOTES

1 Cf. H. Urs von Balthasar, 'L'Evangile comme norme et critique de toute spiritualité dans l'Eglise', in *Concilium*, Nov. 1965, pp. 11–24.
2 J.P. Migne, Pl, 182, 727–808.
3 J.P. Migne, Pl, 732 ff.
4 *Ibid.*, 732.
5 *Ibid.*, 741.
6 *Ibid.*, 749.
7 *Ibid.*, 734.
8 *Ibid.*, 732...
9 Cf. J. Bligh, *Galatians*, St Paul Publications, Slough, 1969.
10 J. Bligh, *op. cit.*, p. 193.
11 Cf.. B. Häring, *Free and Faithful in Christ*, Vol. I, St Paul Publications, Slough, 1978, pp. 225–230.
12 Cf. L. Berg, 'Naturrecht im Neuen Testament', in *Jahrbuch für Christliche Sozialwissenschaft* 9 (1968), pp. 23–42; C. Stuhmüller, 'The Natural Law Question the Bible Never Asked', in *Cross Currents*, 19 (1969), pp. 55–67.
13 Cf. K. Rahner, *Trasformazione strutturale della Chiesa come compito e come chance*, Brescia, 1973.
14 Cf. B. Häring, *Faith and Morality in a Secular Age*, St Paul Publications, Slough, 1974 (with bibliography).
15 Cf. B. Häring, *This Time of Salvation*, New York, 1966, pp. 181–199.
16 From the point of view of anthropology and the sociology of the culture, cf. A. Gehlen, *Moral und Hypermoral: Eine pluralistische Ethik*, Frankfurt/Bonn, 1969; M. Luck, *Das Problem der allgemeingültigen Ethik*, Heidelberg/Löwen, 1963.
17 Cf. H. DeLubac, *Pluralismo di Chiese o unità della Chiesa?*, Brescia, 1973.
18 International Theological Commission, 'Testo Ufficiale sulla fede e pluralismo teologico' (Official text on faith and theological pluralism), in *Settimana del clero*, June 3, 1973, p. 4; Cf. K. Rahner, 'Theological Pluralism and Unity in the Profession of Faith', in *Concilium 5* (1969); J. Müller, 'Missionarische Anpassung als theologisches Prinzip', in *Zeitschrift für Missionswissenschaft und Religionswissenschaft*, Münster, 1973, pp. 1–24; U. Kuhn, 'Die Pluralität der Theologie und die Einheit des Glaubens', in *Theologie der Gegenwart* 16 (1973), pp. 129–139.
19 Cf. A. Auer, *Autonome Moral und Christlicher Glaube*, Düsseldorf, 1971, pp. 123–136.
20 Cf. F. Horst, *Gottes Recht: Gesammelte Studien zum Recht im Alten Testament*, Munich, 1961; J.J. Stamm, *Le Décalogue à la lumière des recherches contemporaines*, Neuchatel, 1969; E. Gerstenberger, *Wesen und Herkunft des 'Apodiktischen Rechts'*, Neukirchen, 1965; A. Deissler, *Die Grundbotschaft des Alten Testaments: ein theologischer Durchblick*, Freiburg/Wien, 1972.
21 Cf. J. Ratzinger, 'Naturrecht, Evangelium und Ideologie in der Katolischen

Soziallehre', in *Christlicher Glaube und Ideologie*, (edited by K. Von Bismarck and W. Dirks), Stuttgart/Mainz, 1964, pp. 24–30; H.V. Daigler, *Heutiges Menschenrechtswusstsein und Kirche*, Köln, 1973.

22 Cf. B. Häring, *Sin in the Secular Age*, St Paul Publications, Slough, 1974, pp. 96–103, pp. 114–123.

23 St Augustine, *De moribus Ecclesiae Catholicae*, lib. I cap. XV, 25, Pl. 32, 1322.

24 Confucius, *Les quatre livres*, translated from the original Chinese into French and Latin by S. Couveur, Ho Kien Fou, 1895, p. 616; Cf. M. Heinrichs, *Die Bedeutung der Missionstheologie, aufgewiesen am Vergleich zwischen den abendländischen und den chinesischen Kardinaltugenden*, Münster, 1954.

25 Cf. H. Bergson, *Les deux sources de la morale et de la réligion*, Paris, 1934, 16th ed.

26 Cf. K. Rahner, *La grazia come libertà*, Roma, 1970; J. Ratzinger, *Il fondamento sacramentale dell'esistenza cristiana*, Brescia, 1971; B. Häring, *The Sacraments in a Secular Age, A Vision in Depth of Sacramentability and its Impact on Moral Life*, St Paul Publications, Slough, 1976.

27 Cf. A. Johnsen, *Responsibility in Modern Religious Ethics*, Washington, 1968; M. Oraison, *Une morale pour notre temps*, Paris, 1964; A. Hortelano, *Morale responsabile*, Assisi, 1968; B. Häring, *Das Heilige and das Gute*, Krailing 1950. Also the introduction to *The Law of Christ*, Westminster, Maryland, vol. I, pp. 35–59.

28 Cf. S. Dunn, *The principle of autonomy in article 36 of 'Gaudium et spes' and in the debate over a specifically Christian morality*, Doctoral thesis, Accademia Alfonsiana, 1972; A. Auer, *Autonome Moral und Christlicher Glaube*, see particularly pp. 153–197.

29 Cf. 'The Protestant Bishop' by H.O. Wöller in *Rheinischer Merkur*, Oct. 16, 1973, p. 29.

30 These basic ideas are presented by J. Grand'Maison, *La seconde évangélisation*, vol. I: *Les témoins*, Montreal, 1973.

31 Cf. *Demitizzazione e morale*, edited by E. Castelli, Roma, 1965.

32 Cf. A. Bengsch, F. Capucci, *'La crisi della società permissiva*, Milan, 1972; S. Lener, 'La crisi della società permissiva', in *Civiltà Cattolica*, 1973, III, pp. 378–389.

33 Cf. A. Revelli, 'Evangelizzazione e scelta dei poveri', in *Note di pastorale giovanile* VII, May 5, 1973, pp. 21–55.

34 Cf. R. Otto, *Das Heilige*, Munich, 1963; B. Häring, *Faith and Morality in a Secular Age*, St Paul Publications, Slough, 1976, pp. 61–73.

35 A. Auer, *op. cit.*, p. 28; the book constitutes a great contribution to the clarification of the problem, but my own approach greatly stresses the complexity of autonomy in relation to sin, and gives more emphasis to the moral exigencies which are influenced by faith itself.

36 Cf. B. Häring, 'Kirchenrecht für eine stationäre Gesellschaft oder für die Pilgergemeinde Gottes?', in *Wort und Wahrheit* 26, (1971), pp. 263–267.

37 Cf. B. Schüller, *Gesetz und Freiheit*, Düsseldorf, 1966; J. Hainze, *Ekklesia-Strukturen: paulinischer Gemeindetheologie und Gemeindeordnung*, Regensburg, 1972; E. Hamel, 'La legge nuova per una comunità nuova', in *Cività Cattolica* III, (1973), pp. 351–360.

38 Paul VI, 'To the participants at the International Congress of Canonists', in *L'Osservatore Romano*, 20 Jan. 1970.

39 K. Rahner, *Trasformazione strutturale della Chiesa come compito e come chance*, (cit.). Rahner offers us a moving picture of this exodus, but also a prophetic vision. He characterizes the evangelization of morals by the title 'Morals without moralizing' (pp. 79–87).

40 This document is quoted according to *Morale di Dio o morale del sistema? La necessità di un'etica a misura d'uomo*, by F.V. Joannes, Verona, 1972, p. 101.
41 Cf. K. Rahner, *Trasformazione strutturale della Chiesa come compito e come chance*, p. 35.
42 Cf. K. Forster, 'Zur theologischen Motivation und zu den pastoralen Konsequenzen der Umfragen zur Gemeinsamen Synode der Bistümer in der Bundesrepublik Deutschland', in *Befragte Katholiken — zur Zukunft von Glaube und Kirche*, Freiburg/Basel/Wien, 1973, pp. 19ff.

PART THREE

EVANGELIZATION AS RESPONSE TO THE *KAIROS*

The Church can respond to the world only in so far as she is completely disposed to listen to the word of God and the word of man, to which she wants to give an answer. Certainly, the Church will bring a message which goes beyond and transcends what man asks. However, man to whom she brings the good news is not a *tabula rasa*: God is always present as Creator and Redeemer. To refuse to pay attention to the signs of the times, to the opportunities and particular difficulties of people, to their ardent search for certain values would mean a refusal to listen to God himself. In evangelization the Church always co-operates humbly with God, the Lord of the history of salvation. Therefore she should meditate not only on the written word of God and her great tradition, but also on all the signs of the divine presence easily found in the world, in order to become the salt of the earth, the light of the world, the leaven in the loaf.

In this third part, I shall try to offer a phenomenology of the world today, in as much as it demands from the Church a particular and serious effort for its evangelization.[1] The reader should remember here how much has been said in the first part about the signs of the times, both positive and negative. What will be discussed now is intended only to complete that picture in the perspective of evangelization and faith-education as a possible concrete response at this moment of history.

1) We preach the gospel to a world which is critical and whose inhabitants do not, as in the past, identify themselves completely either with the Church or with any type of society.

2) We must respond to a world which is extraordinarily dynamic; we can do so only if we know the true dynamism of the gospel.

3) We bring the gospel of liberty and liberation to a world which often thinks itself to be self-sufficient and adult, while

it is threatened by many forms of manipulation and profoundly divided between rich and poor. The gospel will unmask the misery and the existential emptiness of the unjust rich. The Church must accomplish in a new way her mission of the evangelization of the poor in order to be the sacrament of true liberation.

4) We must be fully aware that evangelization addresses itself to a world very different from the one to which the Church proclaimed the gospel and proposed moral norms in the past.

5) We are sent to bring to a polarized and lacerated world the gospel of reconciliation and peace.

NOTE

1 For a fuller treatment and abundant bibliography on the questions of this chapter see B. Häring, *Free and Faithful in Christ*, volume 2: 'The truth will set you free', St Paul Publications, Slough, 1979, pp. 241–378.

1

The response to a critical world

1. *The new situation*

Practically all reflections on the evangelization of the world today concede great importance to the phenomenon which I shall try to clarify in this chapter: the transition from a Christianity profoundly incarnated in the culture in which one was born and educated, to a faith which is a personal choice, often in conflict with the environment. In the past epoch, all were not only baptised, but accepted the Christian reality without any criticism or personal crisis. This is already a thing of the past. Nevertheless, there are still, today, social groups and zones in which a Christianity which can be called 'the Church of the people' continues to exist. The social *élites*, however, and now also parts of the great masses, which are so decisive for the future, are characterized by a personal choice of faith, often after having gone through a more or less long and profound crisis.[1]

In every part of the world there is a considerable group, sometimes the absolute majority of those inscribed in our registers, which is described as 'on the fringe'.[2] These are not completely cut-off from the Church or from a religious tradition, but identify themselves only partially with the Christianity of the past. They do not accept the doctrine of the Church and her moral norms as a package deal to be taken or left. They have, on the contrary, decided to search personally for a synthesis in an existential manner, distinguishing what they can accept and integrate in their plan of life from what does not seem acceptable to them or, at least, is not convincing to them.

The history of dogmatic theology and, with a yet greater clearness, of moral theology shows that the rigorists have always chosen parts of scripture and tradition unilaterally. They were often absolutely blind in the face of the doctrines which were so explicit and insistent on evangelical poverty and evangelical simplicity or on fidelity to an infinitely merciful God, while they were extremely sharp and rigorous in the selecting and explaining of a few words of the Bible regarding, for example, sexual morals or the right to private property. Today this selective attitude towards doctrines is manifested in a different way. It no longer belongs to the schools, lax or rigorous, but to persons or social groups and classes. Pluralism is noted especially among those who truly search for a relation with God, a faith assimilated and integrated into their life. The motive which promotes the choice is no longer a question of schools or external control, but of preoccupation with a coherent and integrated life.

The critical sense, present especially in the young and in some of the socially *élite*, has convinced them that even the clergy has sometimes made wrong and arbitrary choices; and thus with a clear conscience, such persons or groups do not consider their opposing choice as arbitrary, but as existential, and following from a whole and sincere view of things.

In this process of crisis and critical discernment there is often interpolated the phenomenon of reaction, very much evident in anti-clericalism. It is a fact that the clergy has often sought 'faith' in the imposing of a single package: the word of God, but at the same time theological theories with weak foundations and, worse, norms and doctrines originating from political choices, as for example, in the 'sacred alliance' with monarchies or with the upper nobility or, perhaps later, with the bourgeoisie. In the more favourable of the cases the reaction to this state of affairs sought only political and cultural autonomy in confrontation with the clergy. This was good and constituted a most essential part of the phenomenon of secularization. Typical anticlericalism is easily overcome where the clergy and the hierarchy no longer present themselves as the Church or try to impose choices of a political, social, cultural and economic nature. On the contrary, where the clergy still presents itself as the Church and rejects the co-responsibility of the laity, the people of God, while wanting to perpetuate a rough paternalism which mixes the *kerygma* of doctrine and moral norms with a particular subculture or even with political interests, the reaction involves not only anti-clericalism as such but puts in doubt even the teaching in questions of faith and morals, precisely because man finds himself before a mixture, in which he does not succeed in distinguishing easily what is the abiding truth and what is a time-bound formulation or even an unacceptable man-made doctrine.

Good theology has always paid great attention to theological qualifications; so it has distinguished among truth immediately revealed in scripture, truth of defined faith, truth *fidei proximae*, probable doctrine and, finally, theological opinions still discussed or opinions only tolerated. However, unfortunately, in evangelization and in catechesis these distinctions were often not kept in mind and it happened frequently that undue emphasis was given to theories or doctrines that are rather foreign to the faith as such. Critical but sincere men and women of today who have not succeeded in convincing themselves of the exactness of a certain point or of a group of doctrines and moral norms, sometimes as a consequence doubt practically the whole complexus, and so their faith as a whole in the Church enters into a crisis, precisely because those who proposed it to them have failed to make the indispensable distinctions.

Often, the authority of the Church was brought forward as the greatest motive and first support of the faith. And even in problems which, in the strict sense, were not objects of faith, one was prone to speak of the 'obedience of faith'. The world of today is marked by a crisis of authority, which concerns above all the civil and political spheres. All the same, because of alliances with civil society and of a way of exercising ecclesiastical authority very similar to that in which authority is exercised in civil society, the crisis has rapidly spread into the ecclesiastical sphere. This is one of the motives which provoke a world-wide crisis of faith when religious and moral questions are translated into norms of faith, emphasizing rather one-sidedly the authoritative aspect. The crisis deepens and extends when men of the Church, constituted in authority, speak of moral questions invoking the obedience of faith also in problems which do not enter into it, as if nobody remembered the past. There are in fact teachers who are ignorant of the past of the Church, with all its usurpation of competence and prevarication, and are not fully aware of the critical spirit of today.

Another cause of criticism was the militant attitude used by the Church towards other parts of Christianity and against modern culture, especially against the desire for liberty and the affirmation of progress.[3] Again the search for truth by strongly militant members of the various schools was not made in humility, nor did it demonstrate the fruits of the Spirit: benevolence, gentleness, understanding, patience, and so on. To all this was added an apologetic style which could not be an integral or integrating part of evangelization and which made use of motives and methods which have finally revealed themselves as counterproductive.[4]

Thus to the attitude of self-defence assumed as a consequence of the Reformation, counter-Reformation, anti-clericalism, illuminism, materialism and atheism, Church authorities fell often into the temptation to impose everywhere a rigid control: absolutely no formula of the catechisms could be changed; a gradual pedagogy of the faith was not admitted, but it was required that even children should learn difficult metaphysical terms. Again, liturgical and para-liturgical expressions were strictly controlled, and even popular devotions; there was no room for spontaneity in the expression of faith or in prayer. In this way the gap between this religious 'packet' and the personal and social life of many of the faithful became wider and wider. There were many who, unconsciously or consciously, were drawing away from the Church.

This attitude of self-defence and control on the part of Church authorities could appear more or less effective in a closed society, in which Catholicism was still the religion of the state and could use 'the secular arm'. Today, however, the Church finds herself in a time when she has to face and live practically everywhere in pluralistic societies and cultures. Every man and every group must make its own choice between faith and different ideologies, which offer either a religious doctrine or a secularizing mysticism, a way of quasi-salvation. Within this pluralistic society, man must be educated in a critical sense, precisely lest he should see his faith, no longer integrated in a personal and existential plan, collapse.

Dietrich Bonhoeffer described this situation in the slogan: *the world come of age.*[5] The reaction from the traditionalist part of the clergy and laity was of an apologetic nature: it wanted to prove that in fact the world could not call itself adult, and that on the contrary it frequently manifested immaturity; one should not miss the scope of this apologetics: to preserve the traditional methods of control and the paternalistic style in the exercise of authority. Bonhoeffer certainly did not want to assert that the man of today is always mature. On the contrary, what is now manifest is the adult condition of the actual world as *partner* of the clergy and of the Church; so that if it is accused of lack of maturity and of equilibrium it answers with the same tone and the same weapons against the paternalistic clergy.

The situation becomes still more confused through the influence of the fierce waves of world-wide protest in the last decades. Often, we find ourselves before systematic anticonformists who are such because they find themselves ensnared by these waves, thus conforming themselves unconsciously to anticonformism. This facilitates the reactionary attitude of the conservative factions of the clergy and laity, who respond to the protesting world with analogous arguments and attitudes thus reducing the confrontation simply to a fight between contestants.

While the phenomenon of a critical attitude in the confrontation with the Church and her doctrine is practically universal, it manifests itself sharply in particular fields. In these matters there is expressed a candid disagreement not only on the part of those who now for a long time have fallen away, but also on the part of many of those who still participate faithfully in the liturgy and life of the Church, manifesting, rather, a deep solidarity with her.

The most widespread dissent concerns canon law and the effort on the part of ecclesiastical officials to impose on the conscience of the faithful laws and precepts of the past, which at least partially contradict the spirit of the renewal decided by the Church in an official and solemn form. For example, it is sufficient to cite the general dislike and disagreement demonstrated against the system of the ecclesiastical marriage tribunals.[6] In some nations the canonists gave the impression of being a closed and impenetrable cast. Everywhere there was a suspicion that the commission which was preparing the new laws would not accept the necessity — however evident — of inter-disciplinary dialogue and the help of experts who know the actual world and the dynamism of evangelization.

Another interesting fact is that the liturgical renewal has often been able to make headway alone, ignoring or violating firmly established norms of authorities, which finally change them only in view of the accomplished fact. Here it is without doubt a matter of a group of persons very much involved in the life of the Church questioning a certain understanding of authority.

Particularly profound is the criticism of a concept of sin still prevalent among that part of the clergy which laments a pretended loss of the sense of sin among the people, where this often concerns only a change of perspective, often of prophetic character.[7] The hierarchical Church seems to impose absolutely regular attendance at Mass every Sunday and feast day of precept under pain of grave sin, if not outright mortal sin. An ever growing proportion of the clergy expresses doubts on the wisdom of this norm and of the sanctions which accompany it.[8] Many Christians, who do not consider themselves as lax, have formed for themselves on this point a sufficiently firm conscience which does not consider the single fact as a serious sin, let alone a mortal sin.[9]

The most explosive field is, however, that of sexual morals.[10] Because of the encyclicals *Casti Connubii,Humanae Vitae* and of the rigorism with which some wanted to apply its doctrine, millions of Catholics have abandoned participation in the sacraments, some with bad consciences, others on the other hand with the conviction more or less firm that it is the Church that has gone wrong, either in the doctrine itself or, at least, in pastoral praxis. Sociological researches made in many different nations have shown that the dissent does not concern only the question of birth control but also other problems of sexual morals; the dissenters are, however, for the most part persons who as a matter of principle identify themselves with the Church and believe in her divine mission.

The dissent involves not only morals, but also problems of dogmatic nature, as for example the concept of the infallibility of the successor of St Peter. Many doubts and criticisms are expressed also in regard to the doctrine on the eternity of punishment. Often, the disagreement does not hit the doctrine itself, but the obscure and confused ideas which surrounded it.

As far as I can see, many agree with M. Légaut who foresees in questions of faith and of morals a pluralism much larger than the one officially accepted today by the Church, and this not only among the lukewarm and the lax but also among those most engaged and advanced in the spiritual life.[11]

Besides a world that is often too critical or immaturely critical there is another group: it can be called the rear-guard of the Church. It reacts vigorously against criticism of any kind and even against any effort aimed at clearly distinguishing what constitutes the essence of Christianity from what are historically conditioned forms or pious encrustations. This part of the Church, persons who are seeking security rather than truth, frequently exasperates the other side.

2. *The response*

If the Church intends to evangelize the critical world, her response cannot be exclusively theoretical. She must accept this new phenomenon as a sign of the times, a positive opportunity or at least as a challenge which can become salvific.

A. *Following Christ the Prophet*

The first duty is one of a more profound conversion to Christ the Prophet. He with his entire life, and frankly in his words, voiced criticism, even hard criticism, of the situation in which the 'church' of the Old Testament was to be found at his time, shaking above all the conscience of the high priests, the Pharisees and the scribes, and the rich who saw in their privileges a sign of predestination and prerogative in the eyes of God. The Church must deepen in herself the knowledge of Christ the Prophet who lived and taught the synthesis between adoration, knowledge of God, fraternal love and justice. Only if she will accept, in the love of Christ the Prophet, the voices and the criticism of the saints and discover the element of truth which is also somehow in those who are not saints, can the Church become more and more a prophetic voice in the world of today.

B. *The gospel and diplomacy should not be confused*

I consider dangerous and erroneous the bitter criticism of those who call useless and out-dated the institutional aspect of the Church. This does not prevent men of the institution from taking more seriously the constructive points of those who believe in the universal mission of the Church, including her institutional aspect, and who feel compelled to speak by a passionate love which they have for her, and to express constructive criticism and the challenge to accept it.

For example, the criticisms made against the actual structure of the ecclesiastical diplomatic corps should not be ignored.[12] It should not be forgotten that the origin of this structure is not in the gospel, but in a Church of the past marked by the erroneous conviction of possessing direct power in the temporal sphere, and trapped in problems of a political character[12a]. The senior archbishop of the diplomatic corps in a lay state is no longer a figure that can correspond to the self-understanding of the Church and of the world of today. And even if, in itself, it were a question of an acceptable fact, does it not turn out all too easily to be an institutionalized temptation to be less faithful to the mission of evangelizing humbly? The universally critical attitude towards this particular structure alone forces the Church to reflect again on the possibility of finding a more acceptable arrangement, to guarantee on one hand the intimate union between the local Churches and the successor of Peter and, on the other hand, to hold a dialogue of peace and reconciliation with the civil authorities. The Church should represent, even in her institutional structure, an attractive sign of the simplicity and truth of the gospel. Certain forms of diplomatic secrecy, and the Church's ties with worldly diplomacy, easily engender distrust and suspicion; therefore the authorities should have the courage to renew these institutions profoundly in such respects.[13]

C. *An open account of the Church's finances*

Another point which in itself is of minor importance but which touches a tender spot is the administration of the finances of the Vatican and of other ecclesiastical institutions.[14] Every modern state, every administrative unit and every society makes public what it possesses and gives a report of its economic situation in an annual balance-sheet. Though the men in charge of the administration of the goods of the Church might merit the greatest confidence, the Church should remove all the causes of suspicion, because the economic-financial side of affairs should never compromise in any way her credibility. She loses nothing in the publication of her balance-sheet and related facts: on the contrary many will thus be convinced that she is not so rich and will perhaps contribute with even greater generosity towards her needs. The primary attention should however always be given to evangelization, in which effectiveness should never be lessened by trifling questions.

D. *The virtue of discernment*

The most valid and constructive response that could be given to the critical world is, however, special attention to the *virtue of discernment*. We can also call it the *virtue of criticism*.[15] Criticism comes from the Greek term *krisis* and the verb *krinein*, to discern. Man does not arrive at maturity without developing to the maximum in himself the capacity for distinguishing good from bad. Today, in this culture which stimulates and makes criticism necessary, there is the danger that this capacity may degenerate into the *vice* of criticalness. It is therefore useful to cultivate carefully the *virtue* of discernment, the virtue of true criticism.

Criticism is on the road which leads to virtue, when it is exercised before God who is infinitely just and merciful, and when man, before judging others, puts himself under the merciful judgement of God. The virtue of criticism guarantees humility and gentleness in the joint effort to distinguish between that which helps faith, hope, charity and unity, and that which on the contrary is an obstacle to them. Before expressing criticisms in regard to his neighbour or to institutions and communities, a man should praise God for the mercy so many times extended to him. Criticism, when it is a virtue, is always constructive and tends towards the deepening of dialogue. It prefers to raise a query rather than impose a thesis. The contribution towards a joint discernment, therefore, becomes the more effective as a man clearly manifests his solidarity, his respect and his readiness to accept humbly the criticisms addressed to him either from a brother or from one constituted in authority. If it follows these rules, constructive criticism is always directed towards a more mutual dialogue, even when it means disagreement.

Criticism easily becomes a vice and understanding is obscured when it introduces a perfectionism which does not accept the human condition with all its limits, especially the *law of growth*, which means a gradualness in conversion and renewal, inherent in persons as well as in institutions and communities. The perfectionists and the utopians are opposed to continuity in structural transformation, branding it generally as 'reformism', while having recourse with enthusiasm to a vocabulary in which the word 'break-away' (or 'rupture') predominates.

He who does not consider acquiring the virtue of discernment as a primary need is not in a position to preach the gospel. Therefore the virtue of discernment or true criticism must be, in a special way, the distinctive mark of those who dedicate themselves to evangelization and to moral pedagogy.

E. *The necessity of teaching with discernment*

There is need of a clear sense of self-criticism in the proposing of the doctrine and the moral norms of the Church: one must be sure not to preach according to one's own caprice and, as a whole, not to repeat uncritically stereotyped formulations easily alienated from real life. It is a duty, not only of the theologians, but also of all those who are called to evangelization, and according to the charism and competence of each one, to search together for 'more suitable ways of communicating doctrine to people of their times. For the deposit of faith or revealed truth is one thing; the manner in which it is formulated without violence to its meaning and significance is another' (*Gaudium et spes*, 62). [16]

Even where it is a matter of truth of faith, or explicit dogmas, we do not possess formulas which are and which remain perfect and communicable to every new age. If it is compared with other documents of the Holy See, the 1973 declaration *Mysterium Ecclesiae* from the Congregation for the Doctrine of the Faith constitutes a notable progress, because it openly recognizes the necessity of a discernment in regard to formulations depending on a particular culture, language or philosophy.[17] The deposit of the faith is, in the final analysis, confided to the Church not so that she may conserve it in abstract formulas, but so that it may be maintained alive in evangelization and witness to the faith. In this sense orthodoxy can never be separated from evangelization and from the faith that is lived.

To communicate effectively the riches of the faith in its own best interests it is necessary, especially in an age of criticism, to have an acute sensibility to the *hierarchy of truth*.[18] One can avoid confronting people, particularly sceptics, with a decision based on *a posteriori* truth or, worse still, a doctrine deprived of the guarantee of infallibility. He who accepts with ardent faith the central truths and tries to live such a faith will open himself more and more easily to all the other truths which insert themselves as so many voices of one choir. But if the emphasis is put on truths which by themselves alone do not demonstrate the dynamics of salvation, and which cannot show their basic importance, it will finish inevitably by rendering faith more difficult.

F. *The pedagogy of faith*

There is need for the art of pedagogy, in the area of faith as in other areas; for faith often touches the hearts of people through truths and values to which they are particularly sensitive. This, however, would not make it right for such a pedagogy to shift the emphasis to truths which are not at the centre of the apostolic *kerygma* or of a lived Christian life.

Again, out of consideration for those who are critical, one will avoid obscuring or diminishing the mysterious character of faith by over-valuing apologetics or cold reasoning. What should remain constantly fundamental is the joy of faith and the pedagogy of evangelization which can stimulate personal adherence to faith (the *fides qua*).

Cardinal Suenens, when asked the anguishing question, 'What can we affirm today with certainty?' replied: 'Revelation is not a collection of articles each of which is furnished with a certificate of security against all discussion. No, faith is an encounter: God encounters me, and I meet him in prayer and in contemplation. The first letter of St John contains a warning and sometimes a severe accusation against theologians: 'the unloving know nothing of God, for God is love' (1 Jn 4 : 8). If a theologian is not also a contemplative, his doctrine risks remaining superficial.'[18] It is necessary therefore to repeat that the authenticity of the *fides qua* (the total openness to his Truth, and surrender to him) is the primary and fundamental condition which permits a person to arrive at the *fides quae* (the content of revelation).[19]

If a Christian, who believes in Christ and in the mission of his Church, suffers grave difficulties in the case of a single point of doctrine — as, for example, the eternity of the pains of hell — he should search above all to discover the origin of his difficulties, which could perhaps be a rigoristic exaggeration that was threatening hell even for the relatively less serious human weaknesses. But if after all is tried there still remains a diffident opposition the person interested could surely be delicately invited at least to suspend his judgement, continuing in any case to pray to receive light and grace more abundantly. The pedagogy of the faith will know how to take into consideration doubts arising from cultural contexts and especially the fact that many Christians have the same uncertainties or even a firm opposition to certain formulations or unhappy presentations of a specific doctrine.

People of today have read so much about the Church's errors: inquisitions, tortures, burnings of so-called witches, affirmations of the direct power of the pontiffs in every temporal sphere and over all the kings of the earth. Often such facts are publicized with seditious exaggeration, leaving on one side their historical context. All this creates in Christians and catechumens, even of good will, a serious embarrassment, if not exactly about the faith as a whole, at least about some of its doctrines, which cannot be said to belong certainly to the deposit of faith.

In consideration of these many and often new difficulties, the Church must investigate the limits of pluralism[20] of expression and of formulation, not only for the use which she can make of them in theology, but much more, to help those who are, or who want to be members, but are not yet in a position to accept some truths in their lived and convinced faith. There must be the greatest care not to confuse human traditions or philosophical insights or doctrines with revealed truths.

Certainly, undeniable difficulties must not lead us to reduce the *kerygma* or the teaching to only the defined truths. It is necessary always to give a more complete and living picture, without however giving the impression of demanding an assent of faith to doctrines which do not clearly form part of its deposit.[21]

G. *Prophetic parrhesia (boldness) and humility*

Various enquiries have also shown that modern man expects a clear teaching from the Church on moral questions: justice, peace, racism, terrorism, sexual aberration, and so on. But on the level of concrete norms it is easy to meet with reticence or even very hard resistance. If we are aware of the immense and difficult journey made from the morals of the juristic manuals at the beginning of the century to the present biblical and anthropological basis, we should not wonder at the fact that modern man does not willingly accept our precepts and our prohibitions. What then is to be done? Here also the education of discernment should have a central place. First of all a more systematic effort should be made to make Christ himself known and, therefore, true love known, with the power of the final commandment of 'love one another as I have loved you' (Jn 15 : 12). We could also try to offer the true picture of redeeming love, bringing to light the attitudes which essentially contradict such power. Descending then to particular norms, it will not be difficult to recognize, if necessary, the limits of the certainty of some norms which are part of the Church's traditional doctrine, but not of the deposit of faith.

Authority should always have a place of honour in the Church as far as the communication of Catholic doctrine is concerned, because the Church is a community of faith with a magisterium to which was promised the special assistance of the Holy Spirit. But in the pedagogy of faith we must be aware of the fact that many people today are allergic to every shadow of authoritarian argumentation or imposition. 'The institution which wants to impose a static, dogmatic and authoritarian faith will not be listened to.'[22] Difficulties of a psycho-pathological order can however be at least minimized if all ecclesiastical charisms and ministries are put in the right light: the voice of the prophets, the testimony of the saints, the sense of community faith, which have all been lived and translated into existential practice. And surely we must be more ready than ever to offer reasons and convincing motives, to animate and to stimulate rather than to impose imperatives which stifle creativity and liberty of opinion. Besides, it is the educator himself who refuses to develop his own maturity if he acts in a different way.[23] Moral teaching can be very effective even in our critical age if we succeed in showing how the ethical demands — justice, peace,[24] fraternity, unity, mercy, reconciliation and so on — issue from faith in the one God and Father, in the one Redeemer Jesus Christ and in the Holy Spirit who gives life and has spoken through the prophets. The human virtues will thus be presented in a perspective of faith, hope and charity and in the shining light of this perspective.

The Church can never yield to an easy irenicism adjusting her doctrine and her moral message to the spirit of the age. We must preach the evangelical truth without fear and without reticence,[25] also remembering that in the past there were often preached with obstinate insistence many things which were either trivial or obvious errors, while silence was often kept over those fundamental truths which the preachers themselves ignored because they were not ready to live them: mercy, evangelical poverty, renunciation of all spirit of ambition and vanity.

If the Church succeeds in celebrating the faith joyfully and in constructing a community which, in a spirit of intense and vigilant prayer, lives the presence of God and seeks his will in order to put it integrally into practice, then she can hope to be heard even by a critical generation.

NOTES

1 Cf. M. Bellet, *La crisi della fede*, Roma, 1971; B. Häring, 'Crisi di fede e vie di superamento', in *Noi Economi* 4 (1973), pp. 12–15; H. Fries, *Glaube und Kirche auf dem Prüfstand: Versuche einer Orientierung*, Munich/Freiburg, 1970.

2 Cf. P. Lippert, 'Die Fernstehenden. Theologische Deutung eines praktischen Problems', in *Theologie der Gegenwart* 16 (1973), pp. 154–164; R. Zerfass, "Die 'distanzierte Kirchlichkeit" als Herausforderung an die Seelsorge', in *Lebendige Seelsorge* 22 (1971), pp. 249–266.

3 *The Syllabus* of Pius IX (Dec. 8, 1864) concludes with the summary condemnation of the following thesis: 'The Roman Pontiff can and should reconcile and agree with progress, with liberalism and with modern civilization' (Denzinger-Schönmetzer, 2980). This point provoked discussion; it is however obvious that the Church could not accept nor was she bound to accept every idea and form of 'progress' and of liberalism, and she did not even have to canonize modern civilization. This does not take away the fact that her first duty should be to discern and not to react with refusal or universal condemnation.

4 Cf. A. J. Nijk, *Secolarizzazione*, Brescia, 1973, pp. 332–341: 'The paradoxical effect of apologetics'.

5 Cf. A. J. Nijk, *op. cit.*, pp. 69–77.

6 Cf. M. West-R. Francis, *Scandal in the Assembly*, London, 1970.

7 Cf. B. Häring, *Sin in the Secular Age*, Slough, 1974.

8 In his book *Sin in the Secular Age* this author has tried to answer such burning questions as involve morals and the pedagogy of faith. Cf. also the interesting book of Karl Menninger, *Whatever became of Sin?*, New York, 1973.

9 Cf. T. Goffi, 'Non praticano ma l'animo è cristiano: la vita religiosa degli italiani nella valutazione della pastorale di evangelizzazione', in *Settimana del Clero*, Nov. 11, 1973, pp. 4, 8.

10 Cf. E. Kennedy, *What a Modern Catholic Believes about Sex*, Chicago, 1972; G. Baum, 'Catholic Sexual Morality: A New Start', in *The Ecumenist* 11 (1973), pp. 33–40; D. Knab, 'Die Synodenumfrage auf pädagogisch-religionspädagogische Fragen und Ansatzpunkte', in *Befragte Katholiken*, pp. 133–142. Karl Menninger thinks that the fact that auto-erotism (masturbation) was first considered as one of the worst and most dangerous sins and is now looked upon with much greater discernment has induced many to think that in sexual matters sin is gone, *What happened to sin?*

11 Cf. M. Legaut, *Introduction à l'intelligence du passé et de l'avenir du Christianisme*, pp. 151–289.

12 Cf. D. H. Seeber, 'Strategie der Bereinigung' in *Herderkorrespondenz* 27 (1973), pp. 543–546; L. J. Card. Suenens, *La crisi della Chiesa*, IDOC-Documenti nuovi 20, Verona, 1971.

12a Today such criticism is still voiced especially in view of the dwindling Church finances and the huge expenditure involved in maintaining diplomatic missions in a vast number of countries. With the establishment of the Bishops' Conferences on national and regional/continental levels, the apostolic missions have assumed more and more the role of an agent for peace, dialogue and reconciliation between the Church and the State, between the Church and other Christian confessions, between the universal and the local Churches. Cf. canons 364, 365 § 1.

13 The document, *Evangelization of the Modern World*, Part III, I. G.

14 Cf. H. Fleckenstein, in *Befragte Katholiken*, p. 75: It should be noted that 41.6% of the Catholics interviewed who did not go to church mentioned the finances of

the Church as a matter that should be made clear. The answer leaves no doubt that it concerns a sensitive area. Ever since that poll and the first edition of this volume in 1974, Church finances and financial institutions have come under severe criticism, closer scrutiny and drastic re-organization. New vigilance and advisory bodies — "finance committee" and "college of consultors" have been set up from the universal to the local levels in accordance with the demands of the canon law which now requires "all administrators to observe the provisions of canon and civil law; to keep accurate records of income and expenditure; to draw up an account of their administration at the end of each year; . . . to draw up each year a budget of income and expenditure" cf. canon 1284 § 2 : 3, 6–8; § 3 and canons 492–494; 1254–1289.

15 Cf. B. Häring, *A Theology of Protest*, New York, 1970, pp. 55–94.

16 Cf. John XXIII, *Opening Speech of the Second Vatican Council*, 11 Oct., 1962, in *AAS* 54 (1962), p. 792.

17 Cf. A. Dulles, 'Infallibility revisited', in *America*, 4 Aug., 1973, pp. 55–58; K. Rahner, 'Mysterium Ecclesiae: zur Erklärung der Glaubenskongregation über die Lehre von der Kirche', in *Stimmen der Zeit* 191 (1973), pp. 579–594, especially pp. 588ff on the historicity of dogmatic formulation.

18 L. J. Suenens-M. Ramsey, *L'Avenir de l'Eglise,* Paris, 1971, p. 113ff.

19 Cf. L. Monden, *Wie Können Christen noch glauben?*, Salzburg, 1971.

20 Cf. R. Parent, *Condition Chrétienne et service de l'homme: essai d'anthropologie chrétienne,* Montrèal, 1973, pp. 119–152; B. Lonergan, *Method in Theology,* New York, 1972; J. H. Lengsfeld, *Die Alternative zum Terrorismus: Pluralismus in Theologie und Kirche,* Düsseldorf, 1970; A. Dumas, 'Pluralismus in der Kirche?', in *Christliche Freiheit im Dienste am Menschen* (ed. K. Herbert), Frankfurt, 1972, pp. 41–47.

21 Cf. K. Rahner, 'Ist Kircheneinigung dogmatisch möglich?', in *Theol. Quartalschrift* 153 (1973), 103–118. Rahner treats this difficult question in a faith which respectfully leaves suspended an actual judgement in view of the hoped-for union of the Christian Churches. For example, there are many people who consider themselves devout and active members of the Church yet without giving an unconditional assent, let us say, to the dogma of papal infallibility, at least in the form in which it is presented to them.

22 L. Cassiers, 'La foi interrogée par les sciences; conclusions du congrès d'ètudes medico-psychologiques, Luxembourg, 1972', in *Le Supplément* 105 (1973), p. 200. On the consequence of an authoritarian education for the crisis of faith and authority, cf. G. Mendel, *Revolte contre le Père,* Paris, 1972.

23 G. Mendel, *Décoloniser l'enfant,* Paris, 1971, p. 130. 'The adult himself can develop his liberty only in the measure in which it is permitted him from childhood.' This argument is as valid for the pedagogy of faith.

24 Cf. J. Grundel, in *Befragte Katholiken*, p. 65. From the fact that in the enquiry made in the German dioceses 81% of the people interviewed gave greater attention to peace and the relation between faith and peace, it is easy to see how much force an evangelization and a moral pedagogy which follow the biblical message of *shalom* would have.

25 Cf. A. Mazzoleni, 'Le leggi dell'evangelizzazione', in *Evangelizzazione e sacramenti,* Naples, 1973, II ed., pp. 103–124.

2

The response to a dynamic world

1. *The new situation*

I have already cited, in another context, the pastoral constitution *Gaudium et spes* which affirms as one of the characteristic notes of our time the change from a more static vision to a more dynamic one (n. 5). This is a matter not only of theoretical vision, but also of daily and world-wide experience on every level which also causes a new way of looking at life.

As a first point, let us think of the now common knowledge of the great dynamism of the evolution of the cosmos. Catholic apologetics has, unfortunately, resisted for a long time the idea of evolution, in order to affirm on the contrary a static vision not only of the cosmos, but of the existence of man itself and of the order of life. In fact the knowledge of evolution and of the world helps the reading of scripture, which is not an ideology but an account of the history of God's relation with man, an account infinitely dynamic.

One of the most evident and most studied factors of the world of today is the accelerated growth of the population. It is a main cause of so much dynamism and much imbalance. The population explosion would certainly not have been possible without the growth of the sciences, especially of medicine, and without so many discoveries in the technical and economic order. It is difficult to have before us an adequate idea of the growth of the sciences and inventions. One can however safely affirm that actually there exists a greater number of well-trained scientists than all other ages together have produced. Humanity today does not make chance discoveries, but has truly invented the art of invention.

Economic development is a most urgent task, especially for those countries which must face an enormous population growth without yet being sufficiently industrialized. And on the other hand, the capitalist system based on profit imposes a law of continuous expansion so as to be able to conserve the regime of competition, thus being obliged to create new needs all the time, even if they are artificial and even harmful. Our culture is marked by a consumerism. Its demands make the technically developed and richer nations accelerate production and consumption so much that they put the environmental equilibrium in serious danger — with air and water pollution, rapid exhaustion of material resources and so on — while at the same time increasing the technological gap which divides the rich from the poor, so that new imbalances and tensions are always created.

Great also is the growth of the spread and volume of information, which continually inundates the greater part of the globe. The means of social communication have acquired an importance which hitherto was never dreamt of. Such means — radio, television, newspapers, cinemas, records, videocassettes, and so on — have exerted on man new and often disturbing pressures of the psychic and moral order.

Great also is the development of scholarship and of the needs of professional specialization. Everywhere new universities with new disciplines are founded. These universities are the source of many imbalances and of a dynamics both positive and negative. A one-sided orientation towards specialization often neglects the total formation of man. The access to cultural goods is now possible for the majority of people, while in the past it was the privilege of few. But the vision of wholeness and a spiritual formation are not offered to the same degree.

A most rapid transformation of customs is due to the influence of technology on every form of life, even agricultural life, and above all to the phenomena of urbanization and of the new great nomadism (tourism, emigration).

Dialogue grows on all levels in international relations and between various cultures, religions and ideologies.

All this gives constructive opportunities and possibilities which till now were unthinkable, but which also provoke imbalances on all levels and which manifest themselves in the inability to discover the true power of spiritual life, and in harmful phenomena of the psychological order, for example: drug abuse, violence, terrorism.

2. *The response of the gospel to the dynamic world*

To know or perceive the dynamic nature of the world of today already forms part of evangelization, because we can thus insert ourselves in the dynamic plan of God, Creator and Redeemer.[1] But if we want to give an evangelizing response we must reflect on the authenticity of those who announce the gospel. While it is necessary always to keep alive an awareness of the questioner — the world of today with its dynamics — we cannot give up that which is rather more important, the message to be communicated, the prophetic nature of which will unmask the falsehood disentangling itself from so many of the pressures on modern man. We have a dynamic gospel which, if we know how to present it well as witnesses, can touch the hearts of the best men and women of this our age.

A. *Re-assessment of the sense of dynamic movement*

To win persons and groups who are distinguished by their dynamic temperament, in tune with the mental and social structures of our age, is of paramount importance for the future of the world and the Church, much more than to give tranquilizing assurance to fearful and timid souls who look for nothing other than a static security. All the same it seems that different people of good will and high quality hate the idea which incites development, change and dynamism because they find themselves before so many propositions truly discouraging and dangerous. To win both the one and the other group we must re-assess the sense of dynamism, that is, denounce that false dynamism which blatantly searches for what is sensational, the new just because it is new, developing misguided aims, and turn our eyes to the dynamic presence of God in salvation history.

The spiritual forces of man have not kept pace with his economic, technical and scientific development, either in the west or in the communist world.[2] The ruthless mechanism of economic-commercial expansion has often subordinated man to profit. This becomes evident in the excessively influential role now assumed by the big possessors of capital and by the directors of their firms or, in communist countries, by the bureaucratic administrators of production. It is sufficient, as examples, to think of the car industry which is expanded according to these rules, not paying any heed at all to the traffic now congested in the cities nor to the enormous number of human lives lost every year on the roads, a number which is certainly superior to that of the major wars of old.

When man's dynamism is exhausted one-sidedly in the technical, productive and commercial field, in a word in making profit, man loses his sense of wholeness and, at least partially, his most noble capacities: admiration, adoration, spiritual awareness and responsiveness. In this way, man, who has even given proof of great technical capacities and has reached economic success, often falls sick and suffers, because of his existential emptiness, of noogenic neurosis (noogenic: existential in origin). Evangelization, or perhaps pre-evangelization, must convince people that they will remain or become more underdeveloped if they are unable or unwilling to impose limitations and wise measures in the face of technico-material development. To one who already feels an existential vacuum, we must offer the values of true leisure, the sense of silence, so that he can enter into the sanctuary of his own conscience in the depths of which he will feel the presence of God. He must free himself from the industry which organizes his leisure time for profit, to be able truly to recreate himself and find himself again in a right relationship. We must offer oases of contemplation, schools of prayer, zones and moments of silence which prepare for the profound experience of the true value of things, a taste for things spiritual, which also give, in fact, sense to everyday life and to every type of life: economic, cultural, political, scientific, social, and so on.

Intensifying the dynamism of radical change in areas of technique, of economic organization and, above all, of sensational reports is a matter of simple acceptance, on the part of many people, of a language of breaks with the past favourable to violent revolutions to the methods of terrorism and to a destructive use of persons. It will be possible to un-mask and denounce this most erroneous dynamism (which leads inevitably to disaster) only if a considerable number of the social and religious *élite* find the synthesis between contemplation and life, between exploration of the inner space and a vision of the history of humanization, through a faith and prayer which render persons and groups capable of a non-violent and solid action, and of the patience which does not lose energy uselessly, but which gathers together every passion and creativity in peaceful commitment to a more fraternal world.[3]

B. *The law of grace*

Those who live the gospel will be in a position to keep the world for what can be made and organized in proper dimensions so as to be able to regain the *sense of gratuity and of gratitude*. Whatever man does — whether it be regarding even the most admirable foundations and successes, as in the conquest of the moon and other planets — it will not have lasting value for those who lose that sense of gratitude which opens on to wider and loftier horizons. The virtue of gratitude should therefore be cultivated also in relation to tradition and the experience and co-reflection of all the previous generations. Furthermore, we must deepen in ourselves the capacity for admiring what is good, for enjoying it, and sensing even better the facets and depths of beauty, that is the splendour of truth and goodness.

The Old and New Testaments offer us a magnificent expression of what is true, good and beautiful as the *glory of God* which radiates itself in all his works and in the events of the history of salvation. God makes believers feel the signs of his presence touching them with grace. They live religion and find the synthesis of life and an authentic equilibrium in the awareness of the *mysterium tremendum* and of the *mysterium fascinosum*. In this way the truly religious person discovers in what is beautiful, in what is true and in what is good dimensions which remain hidden or impenetrable to one who uses practically all his energy for a successfully organized world.

Besides the concept of the *glory of God* there is that of *grace (charis)*, which is the infinitely generous God drawing us to himself, the God who makes us experience the gratuity of his peace, justice, love (*agape*) and reconciliation with himself and among ourselves. For evangelization, it is very important not to take as a starting point a concept of grace that is too abstract or practically materialized. Grace should rather be presented biblically as a dynamic relation of the glory of God which invites us to grateful love and which can be said to be accepted when we know how to adore God in holy fear and with joy.

The actual world cannot be liberated and redeemed without the evangelizers themselves having a profound experience of gratuity. And this is possible only in a life which is inserted in the dynamism of praise and thanksgiving.

When the disciples returned from their first mission in which they proclaimed the joyful news and prepared the way of the Lord, there was a great joy in them and Jesus rejoiced in the Spirit and gave thanks to the Father, Lord of heaven and earth, because he had revealed the great mysteries to little and simple people (cf. Lk 10 : 21). As a preparation for the Christians' task of being heralds of the gospel, of peace and reconciliation, a serious education in prayer of praise and of thanksgiving is indispensable so that they can affirm existentially the gratuity of God's gifts; for this leads to a mission accepted with joyous enthusiasm. St Paul begins practically all his letters and every essential point in them with such a prayer. Such a spirituality made him perceive with a unique intensity the urgency of evangelization. Since the knowledge of Christ was given to him gratuitously, although he was earlier a persecutor of the disciples, and since he considered the knowledge of Christ, inseparable from the total gift to him, as the greatest grace, he could under no condition whatsoever renounce the evangelization of the world. In fact, the actual situation of dynamism which proceeds in the wrong direction, provoking imbalances and tensions, makes the conversion to gratuity more urgent, not only in consideration of the indispensable qualities of the evangelizer, but also of the world which loses itself if it does not find witnesses to grace and the law of grace.

It is not possible to communicate the gospel of grace without accepting and living its inner dynamics. 'For sin shall no longer be your master, because you are no longer under law, but under the grace of God' (Rom 6 : 14). Scientific moral theology, and especially moral pedagogy, must be watered from this source.

The authentic sense of responsibility before God and men springs from the gratuity of the divine gifts: thus each of us, in every instant of life, will ask, 'How can I give back to the Lord all that he has given to me?' (Ps 115). In this manner those in authority and the entire Church will renounce uniformism and the mean and hard controls of meticulous laws. The whole moral vision of the disciples of Christ, particularly of those consecrated to evangelization, should reflect the parable of the talents. A moral system by which only legally imposed observance is considered obligatory deprives the Church of dynamism and grace. It is however clear that it is not possible to teach the law of grace if the gospel does not take first place. Morality should never proceed according to schemes of law *and* grace or of law *and* gospel, but rather always in a vision of responsibility to the gospel and gratitude for grace, which process alone becomes a total and grateful response.

C. *The power of faith and the law of faith*

In view of the evangelization of every culture and nation, Paul the apostle of the Gentiles stressed that it is not the Judaic law which brings salvation, and that justification through faith is for all a gratuitous gift. 'For all alike have sinned, and are deprived of the divine splendour, and all are justified by God's free grace alone, through his act of liberation in the person of Christ Jesus. . . . For our argument is that a man is justified by faith quite apart from success in keeping the law' (Rom 3 : 23–28). In the conflict with the Judeo-Christian moralists—desirous to impose uniformly the traditions, customs and laws of their nation—Paul insisted very much on a morality that would follow the outlook of gratuitous justification through faith. This way of talking was difficult for Jewish moralists to understand, even for those who were very sincere. The apostle had to convince them that teaching as he was doing was not a lowering of morality, but rather on the contrary, a strengthening of it, by orientating it the right way, putting it on the right basis. To those contradicting him he responded passionately: 'Does it mean that we are using faith to undermine morality? By no means: we are placing law itself on a firmer footing' (Rom 3 : 31). As is often the case in his letters,

Paul rather plays on the term 'law', 'order', *nomos*. For him it signifies first of all that which constitutes the synthesis of the covenant: the redeeming and gratuitous love which obliges man to love with gratitude, generosity and mercy. It concerns the law written in the heart, of the Gentiles also, of which he has spoken in the preceding chapter (cf. Rom 2 : 12–16), and which is expressed in the tradition of the Old Testament and of the good pagans in the golden rule: 'Do to your neighbour what you would like to be done to you', or 'Love your neighbour as yourself'.

This old law now finds a completely new dynamism in the love shown us by Jesus; the new measure and intention are essential: 'Love one another as I have loved you'. Paul reaches the summit with the hymn to the 'law of the Spirit (that) has set you free from the law of sin and death' (Rom 8 : 2). Thus are fulfilled the great messianic prophecies which speak of the covenant and of the new law inscribed in the heart by the Spirit, or of the law which God gives to us, communicating to us his own Spirit. Here, in Romans 3, Paul, while speaking of the gratuity of justification and of justifying faith, introduces a completely new concept: *'the law of faith'*. He who receives faith with a right disposition, gratefully and joyfully giving himself to God with unlimited confidence, will in fact discover through it the new law written in the experience of faith and in the heart. For the apostle a faith transformed into an abstract doctrinal system is inconceivable. Faith for him is the response to the gospel, given in thanksgiving and finally in the Eucharist when Christians unite themselves to the thanksgiving of Christ himself and thus receive the divine energy to bear fruit in love, in peace and in reconciliation for the life of the world. I hope I do not weary the reader by returning so many times to this point, which is central and should be observed from every angle and in every perspective: faith is a tree to bear fruit and before one would educate according to a code of laws, however just they may be, it is necessary to offer a pedagogy of faith in which should be integrated every type of moral education, because it is always possible to know Jesus Christ, the message of the Father, and the plan of the Father for the world better and better.[4] Thus the tree will become good and our life will bear good fruits.

Against the disoriented and reactionary dynamism of secularism and horizontalism, we need especially employ to advantage the dynamism of faith which preserves us from all degrading deviations. Certainly we must recognize without hesitation and without reservations the relative autonomy of men, particularly of experts in various fields. But this does not mean that we can make experiments in the moral field ignoring the explicit faith or even the analogy of faith, or intentionally ignoring for a moment that Christ alone is truth and light. Actually we are witnessing the appearance of a morals which considerably exalts its own autonomy by attributing a practically secondary place to the intentionality that comes from faith. However, the threat which diminishes the light of faith and its dynamism when fundamentalists refuse to integrate into the vision of faith the dynamism of history, culture and shared experience and also reflections made by Christians, or in general, by men of good will, is not less grave. In any case the mystery of sin, and therefore the restricted value of human experiences which are foreign to the light of faith and are deprived also of an implicit faith, must not be ignored. A morality which has not at least the character of *analogia fidei* and is therefore not ready to enter fully into the dynamics of faith has no value for salvation.

The pedagogy of the faith as the condition and intrinsic force of continuous conversion finds its culmination in the liturgy and in the universal education to prayer as presence and listening, as watchfulness and readiness to receive the mission with a 'Lord, here I am, send me!'[5] If the Church is truly, as the Lord wanted her to be, a house of prayer, individual and community prayer, especially in liturgical celebration, will be a source of joy, of faith and of missionary readiness. 'I will bring them to my holy mountain and give them joy in my house of prayer. Their offerings and sacrifices shall be acceptable on my altar; for my house shall be called a house of prayer for all nations' (Is 56 : 7). The celebrations of 'the sacraments of faith' are by nature pastoral and missionary. If these celebrations lack this aspect, then we must look for the cause of it in our own faults, in ritualism and lack of personal and family prayer.[6]

D. *The dynamics of the law of the Spirit*

I have no intention of pausing for long here to treat this aspect, because I have done so in all my books during the last twenty years. I cannot however completely pass this perspective by in a synthesis in regard to evangelization.

The dynamic people of today will never accept a system of mere imperatives and moral doctrine, even if all were rightly explained. If the witnesses of the gospel do not live according to the Spirit, they will not succeed in liberating the human person; not even the truest doctrine or the wisest of legal codes (cf. Rom 7) can bring wholeness in itself. The song of the redeemed exalts the law of the Spirit which frees them from that terrible law of being part of those who are bound up with the solidarity of sin and constantly threatened by the fear of death (cf. Rom 8 : 2). A life according to grace, in faith and in docility to the Spirit, loosens us from the strings of the letter of dead formulation, giving back to us that spontaneity which makes us co-operators with God, Creator and Redeemer.

We must not be afraid of the spontaneity of authentically spiritual persons who live their spirituality, necessarily, in and for the community, because the fruits of the Spirit bring us to true unity and solidarity.[7]

The dynamism of 'the law of the Spirit' makes the redeemed hear the cry of all creation, which longs to have a share in the freedom of the children of God who have involved themselves together in permeating all the structures of life with justice, peace, and new liberty (cf. Rom 8 : 9–17).

A true dynamism of the renewal of the Church and of society cannot be foreign to the law of the Spirit, which renews both the heart and the face of the earth. The moral life which is the fruit of the Spirit (cf. Gal 5 : 21–23) is identical with the morality of the beatitudes. Conversion and authentic renewal issue from the joyful news of the paschal mystery and from the pentecostal event which unites us to the risen Christ and makes us live according to the law of grace and of the Spirit.

A dynamism of this sort is to be found, at least partially, in the movement begun by the monks of Taizé, in many groups of pentecostal Catholics, Anglicans and Methodists (the charismatic renewal), in the international movement of 'the house of prayer', in the *Focolarini* and in many other movements and communities which want to express in their life and in their own structures faith in 'the Holy Spirit who gives us life and has spoken through the prophets'. To this dynamism also belong, necessarily, the earthquakes and the shocks provoked by obedience to the Spirit and by the acceptance of prophetic voices, often discomforting, which detach us from false security and invite us to a greater readiness for new opportunities.

E. *The dynamics of hope*

Hope is the dynamic structure of the faith and charity of the pilgrim Church through which every new gift and all new knowledge become a call to proceed on the journey with God, to make the exodus from the limited world which looks for security in its own works and constructions. In hope the believers confide themselves to God who came, comes and will come. In the very desert of detachment, therefore, in the necessity to change and to take the risk of the law of the Spirit and the ever higher demands arising from it truthful adorers will witness to the presence of the Lord and Redeemer of human history.

Modern man has discovered the supremacy of the future over the past, not so much in theory but in the will to self-determination and to transform the world surrounding him. What testimony or meaning does Christian hope give to this approach? E. Schillebeeckx answers, 'Since the future is a free gift of God — a gift which as Christians we must already interiorize now in our earthly history — the eschatological hope will always be a critical protest against every position which pretends to assert that the future as a totality could be the object of only technological activity.'[8]

Christian hope indicates the presence of the Holy Spirit. It is like a storm for the one who puts his confidence in his own capacities of organization and activity, as if that would be the only thing that counts.[9] In it the believer renders thanks to God for all his works and especially for the promises granted to us in the paschal mystery and in the effusion of the Spirit. In this hope the disciples of Christ find the courage to live in the continuous need of becoming, or correcting themselves, of converting themselves and of renewing structures, waiting however for the ultimate and definitive fulfilment from God alone, and making every step in the confidence that the generous response to the signs of God's presence opens the true horizon of the immediate future and of the absolute future.

In hope, the Christian accepts the existing situation of conflict in this world, not in order to aggravate it, but rather in order to be an active presence of the messianic peace, which has the force of renewing the meaning of suffering and of partial defeats. It is possible to find this new meaning of suffering, of persecution and death in Christian hope because it is a presence of the paschal mystery. It is, however, not possible to look for such a meaning in flight or in any form of evasion. The hope for a new earth and a new heaven can never neglect vigilance for the opportunities of the present moment.

Christian hope has its source in prayer, in praise of the marvels which God has accomplished, in supplication for grace, and in meditation which fuses with a discernment of the signs of the times.[10]

F. *The dynamics of natural law and of conscience*

The moral life and the moral doctrine of Christians can never make transparent the dynamics of grace, of faith, of the law of the Spirit, of hope and of vigilance if a static concept of the natural law is opposed to them, as unfortunately was the case in a great many of the Catholic schools.

Believers do not need to cling to a code of formulas and of artificially manufactured norms, precisely because the God of revelation has clearly indicated to them the scope and direction of the journey to be covered, at least in its main lines. The tradition and the wisdom which are expressed among great thinkers, Christian and non-Christian, and especially among humble people, are highly appreciated, but we cannot on account of this think that we have now reached a perfect and complete knowledge of the norms of the natural law. Man is a historical being: he has a history which he must continually mould and remake with material which he receives from the past and which he uses in view of the future. It belongs to our very nature to be on the march and to search with perseverance and in solidarity with all people for the meaning of present history in the light of the past and in view of responsibility for the future.[11]

One can speak of natural law only if one speaks at the same time of the dynamics of *conscience*[12] and that of dialogue.[13] St Paul presents the natural law to us as a law of love and solidarity inscribed in the heart of the person who searches in his conscience for that which is just and true (cf. Rom 1:12–16). The natural law is not manifested in the platonic heaven of immutable ideas or of fixed concepts in formulas that are thought to be immutable. The natural law is the historical reality of people who live in community, share their experiences united to others in reflection. It is only in fidelity to the dynamics of conscience and in full openness to others according to historically possible horizons of dialogue that people can gradually discover the demands of the natural law. 'In fidelity to conscience, Christians are joined with the rest of men in the search for truth, and for the genuine solution to the numerous problems which arise in the lives of individuals and from social relationships. Hence the more a correct conscience holds sway, the more persons and groups turn aside from blind choice and strive to be guided by objective norms of morality' (*Gaudium et spes*, 16).

Divine revelation and magisterial charism do not dispense Christians from this openness and from the dynamics of the dialogue of people who search together for the truth in conscience. Conscienceness of insertion in the history of salvation and faith in the presence of God in his entire creation and in the whole of history become a new motive for dialogue. Where Christians follow the law of the Spirit they will be distinguished by their readiness to listen and to encourage a respectful and mutual dialogue: 'The Lord God has given me the tongue of a teacher and skill to console the weary with a word in the morning; he sharpened my hearing that I might listen like one who is taught. The Lord God opened my ears and I did not disobey or turn back in defiance' (Is 50 : 4–5).

Paul VI, who so happily chose the theme of evangelization for the synod of bishops in 1974, had with his first encyclical, *Ecclesiam suam*, committed himself to the course of dialogue.

This dialogue will be pre-evangelization only if it becomes a force and power for conversion and renewal within the Church and in the ecumenical movement.[14] The power of dialogue is the law written in the heart of the Church, because the Holy Spirit who rules and unites her with his many gifts, charisms and works, is himself her life breath (cf. *Lumen gentium,* 32). The Spirit works in all and for the good of all. Shared meditation with spontaneous prayer of praise and thanksgiving, times of silence as a condition for listening and responding, show the purpose of dialogue among the faithful who in their diversity and reciprocity of conscience are united in their search for the signs of the presence of God, and profit by the opportunities thus offered them (cf. Eph 5 : 16).

But the spiritual aspect of dialogue does not exempt us from the use of means available to all. It rather binds us in a particular manner to use these means. Here I should like to stress only the study of the behavioural sciences, especially of the dynamic processes of social relations, whose knowledge is now indispensable. Those who are sent to proclaim the good news should make use of the dynamics of the mass media and try to discover all the actual forces and opportunities to broaden and to deepen their freedom. The ineffectiveness of a scholastic system which does assert freedom but does not keep contact with the important experiences and reflections undergone by people of today is only too obvious.

NOTES

1 Cf. J. Rossel, *Mission in a Dynamic Society,* London, 1968.
2 In regard to this one can see the prophetic protestation of a man who has often surprised many with his analysis of the world of today. I. Ilich, *Tools for Conviviability,* New York, 1973.
3 Cf. B. Welte, *Die Dialektik der Liebe,* Frankfurt, 1973; the second part of the book treats of 'Christian love in a technological culture'.
4 Cf. F. X. Durrwell, *Le mystère pascal, source de l'apostolat,* Paris, 1969.
5 Cf. B. Häring, *Prayer: Integration of Faith and Life,* St Paul Publications, Slough, 1975.
6 Cf. B. Häring, *This Time of Salvation,* New York, 1966, pp. 123–170; H. Fleckenstein, in *Befragte Katholiken,* p. 79, in his reflections on the enquiry made among the German dioceses came to this conclusion: 'it seems to me that the material collected gives a weighty judgement on the "missionary" force of the liturgical resources of our parishes.'

7 Cf. D. Grasso, 'Evangelizzazione e testimonianza della comunità', in *Evangeliz-zazione e sacramenti*, Naples, 1973, 2nd ed., pp. 124–133.

8 E. Schillebeeckx, 'For an Image of God in a Secularized World', in *La Secolariz-zazione* (the Italian text by S. Acquaviva and G. Guizzardi), Bologna, 1973, p. 283.

9 Cf. F. Hahn, 'Der Braus Gottes', in *Neues Glaubensbuch* (ed. by J. Feiner and L. Vischer), Freiburg, 1973, pp. 235–245.

10 Cf. B. Häring, *Hope is the Remedy*, St Paul Publications, Slough, 1971.

11 A. Müller, S. Pfürtner, B. Schnyder, *Natur und Naturrecht: Ein interfakultäres Gespräch*, Freiburg, 1972; A. H. Maslow, *The Further Reaches of Human Nature*, New York, 1973, 3rd edition.

12 C. E. Nelson (editor), *Conscience: Theological and Psychological Perspectives.* Basic writings by the key thinkers in theology and psychology, New York/Paramus/Toronto, 1973.

13 Cf. C. Curran, *Catholic Theology in Dialogue*, Indiana, 1972; F. Gneo, *Educazione al dialogo*, Rome, 1971.

14 Cf. W. A. Visser't Hooft, 'Dynamic Factors in the Educational Situation', in *The Ecumenical Review* 21 (1969), pp. 320–337.

15 Cf. G. Deussen, *Ethik der Massenkommunikation bei Papst Paul VI*, Paderborn, 1973, which studies the means of social communication following the thinking of Paul VI, always with evangelization in mind.

3

The evangelization of a world
in need of liberation

1. *The situation*

Nothing is clearer to the social *élite* of the contemporary world than the value of liberty and of engagement in the work of liberation. There are many motives for this. Man has found the means and capacities for liberating himself from the numerous conditionings which bound him in the past and came to be accepted as 'necessary' or 'divine' providence. On the other hand, he suffers new anxieties and threats to his most essential liberty, since, not having developed his spiritual liberty to the same extent, he feels himself manipulated in the unlimited use of his technical and scientific capacities.

Everyone speaks of liberty. But this term certainly does not have the same meaning in the communist world as it has in the west. Furthermore, in every part of the world there are great differences in the many meanings given to this same term. Dialectical materialism holds that the total liberty of humanity will increase with the growth of *homo faber* and the concentration of all energy in favourable economic structures. Liberalism, which ideologically conditioned classical capitalism, supports a similar vision; it strangely thinks that the economic world does not need any ethical or juridical norms, and that industrial expansion and material well-being could, with the operative conditioning of the law of profit, bring the greatest happiness to all people even if there would be difficult moments for the great masses.

Already in the past century the philosophy of progress too naïvely bound the idea of liberty to a progressive vision as an almost automatic law of history and evolution. Today, the world perceives the deep gap that lies between development and humanization, and between material prosperity and liberty. We all now stand at a cross-roads, and we must decide which type of liberty and development we want to choose for our future.

At first it looked as if science had found the key to every form of development, and after a century that has seen such technico-mathematical feats, we now find ourselves confronted with unheard of opportunities in the biological and medical fields. Will we be able to make a good use of them? Still more, this world, so rich and powerful, feels more than ever its own misery in the face of rich nations and social classes which live in untold luxury while the number of those who are not only poor but even lack the bare necessities of life increases. In fact, the gap which divides rich from poor does not show any signs of narrowing, but rather broadening, thus inevitably provoking the growth of tensions which cause renewed explosions of hatred and violence. Besides, only a blind person will fail to see the spiritual poverty of the rich and powerful of today. One of the most evident examples is in the small white minority groups in South Africa. They annually increase their wealth, luxury and military arsenal, while at the same or at an even more accelerated speed, their anxiety and their loss of human dignity before millions of shamefully exploited and neglected human beings grows.

The world is becoming smaller; it is therefore more difficult for the rich nations and classes to remain in their egoism and assume a heedless attitude towards the requests of the majority who justly claim their share in the use of human resources.

The growth of scientific knowledge and the unlimited use of it by a small minority that is incapable of freely imposing on itself a decent measure of material prosperity, lead to the constant growth of atmospheric and environmental pollution and to a rapid exhaustion of human resources. If mankind does not find spiritual liberty and also a new moral liberty in the use of technique and methodology the total collapse of the environment will be inevitable. Man who thought he could dominate the earth with technique and economico-industrial expansion, is now moving towards self-destruction if he is not ready to seek a totally new orientation. A qualitative change is necessary.

A part of the rich nations and classes thinks it can solve the problem of the future by means of massive abortion. But it fails to realize that once it has taken such a road, it will no longer be possible to avoid the general growth of violence, terrorism and anxiety, which movements are difficult to stop once they are in motion. Besides the fact that a different style of life will be imposed once the essential resources are exhausted and an ecological collapse occurs, man will find himself spiritually unprepared to solve problems in the light of world solidarity. He will probably fall into the horrible snares which will be the culmination of his own egoism and the lust for power and arrogance. In fact, it is easy to observe how the unilateral growth of the *homo faber* has been in equal pace with the existential void and the new slavery of the individual and the entire community who sedulously adore the tribal and market idols.[1]

It is true that the immense power of the means of social communication has given man a valuable help, because man can now liberate himself from the narrow tribal outlook through better information and more ample dialogue. But as these means are practically all in the hands of nations and classes marked by their arrogance, founded on egoism and materialism, even though these means may be so precious in themselves, they become a continuous snare both for the manipulated and the manipulators. They are used not only for a bombarding publicity which increasingly creates new and artificial needs for materialist man, but also to guide people in more delicate questions and fields in a culture in which the market and the law of the stronger dominate; the communication of ideas even becomes an ideological cult and directly influences public opinion in regard to culture, and worse, in matters of morals and religion.

The picture painted here surely looks dark and sad. It would however not be exact to fail to see also the signs of hope contained there: precisely because the wise perceive the danger which threatens people, the spiritual energies of many who are searching for liberty are also awakened. There are the social *élite* who are re-discovering the meaning of contemplation and a new sensitivity which alone will allow a genuine action for the maintenance of liberty and liberation. Whoever sincerely looks for liberty and its true meaning, and is ready to join others in overcoming the conditions and eliminating the ideologies which are obstacles to his liberty, is truly a sign of hope and a reason for confident optimism. There is also a new sensibility towards the human rights due to everyone: mankind will have everything to gain when we understand that we cannot enjoy our liberty if we do not use all powers of wisdom for the liberty of all.

2. *Evangelization as a liberating response*

We cannot possibly evangelize the contemporary world without being aware of the situation of a manipulated world; strange as it may seem, both manipulators and manipulated of this world, confined to the horizons of the makeable and the operative conditions necessary for it, have to decide for themselves in favour of either universal liberation or complete slavery.

A. *The Church, the sacrament of liberty and of liberation*

The Church cannot remain faithful to the Lord of history who has sent her to evangelize the modern world if she does not teach the values which are peculiar to the liberty by which Christ has liberated us.[2] The entire life of the Church, her celebrations and the proclamations of the good news, the pedagogy of the faith and the formation of conscience, in short, everything, must be a great sign of liberty and a commitment to true liberty and for liberation. 'Action for justice and participation in the transformation of the world are clearly coupled as the constitutive dimension of the preaching of the gospel; that is to say, they are together the constitutive dimension on which is based the mission of the Church for the redemption of the human race and its liberation from every state of oppression.'[3]

The Church will engage herself in the liberation of all men at all times and at all levels in the measure that she is conscious of the gratuity of the liberty of salvation and also in the measure that she is aware of the greatness of this gift. The affirmation that the Church is, in Christ, the great sacrament of salvation might be translated as follows into modern language: the Church is instituted by Christ so that she, being grateful for the gift of liberty, may present herself to the world as a visible and efficacious sign of the integral liberation of humanity.[4]

Liberty is confided to the community and to each one in the community so that the entire human race may participate in it. It is confided as a seed which must develop, but which is always threatened by sin, particularly by egoism, pride, and individual as well as collective indolence. Man cannot live his call to liberty in any sphere whatever without the gift of redemption, which is liberation from the power of sin. 'The mission of the Church is fundamentally and primarily ordained towards liberation from sin and death, and towards a reconciliation of men among themselves in Jesus Christ' (cf. *Gaudium et spes*, 13; 18; 32; 92). But it also embraces liberation from all human slavery — economic, political, social, cultural — which 'derives ultimately from sin' (*Gaudium et spes*, 41).[5] When the Church lives and communicates the gospel, she renders a specific contribution to the liberation and total liberty of people. This contribution is one which goes beyond the horizons of purely human experience. So there is not just a simple identification between evangelization and the promotion of social liberation, but one cannot admit a dichotomy. In every age and cultural or social context, a concrete integration and continuity must stand out.[6] This is a matter of education for wisdom.

The mission of the Church is to continue that of Christ, who was anointed and sent by the Spirit to proclaim the good news and to restore liberty to the oppressed and prisoners (cf. Lk 4 : 18). Thus her mission is undivided and is indivisible: it concerns the total liberation of all in all its dimensions. The Church therefore has to consider, in the first place, the totality of the gift and the promises confided to her; the readiness to accept the mission to be witness and instrument of a liberty that liberates comes from the gift.

It is a point that takes precedence for the Church to verify whether in all her life she has presented herself credibly as sacrament and servant of the liberty of all. She cannot rejoice in the gift of the liberty which is salvation if she is not completely consecrated to the service of the liberty which is liberation, and the salvation of all humanity. The Church can accept liberty only in its totality, that is without reserve and without making unjust discriminations and limitations. She cannot uphold and communicate it in evangelization if she does not first of all live it in the context of her whole life, in, for instance, the ecclesiastical press, in the use of canon law, in administration, in the organs of collegiality and so on. On the other hand, it remains true that the Church will never live internally in a growing liberty in the sense of liberation without at the same time being preoccupied with and working for the liberty of the human race at every level: domestic, economic, cultural, social, political, and so on.[7]

There is a profound interdependence between the degree of liberty present in the secular world and the Church's ministry. In her task the Church is helped and encouraged by existing liberty insofar as it is truly desired by the culture to which she addresses herself, whereas her action is often aborted and even her internal relations remain handicapped if in that social context liberty is despised and obstructed. Here it is sufficient to think of the history of the Inquisition and torture: the Church had for a long time defended herself against these phenomena, but was finally corrupted by them when the influence of society became ever stronger. This offers a further reason for always engaging herself in a complete and integrated effort for the liberty which is liberation.

Real liberty, that is liberty realized, incarnate and situated in the Church and in the world, is a promise, hope and appeal to use and increase its own capacity. The message of the Church is not first of all an imperative: live the liberty! liberate yourselves! Rather, the specific contribution of the Church is the gospel. Christ has freely liberated you so that you can live as free persons and fulfil your mission of creative and redemptive liberty so that it may permeate the world.

The gospel that the Church communicates to the world is that of the final eschatological liberation, without which it would not be possible to understand exactly the liberty which is already in act and concerns us. However, the message of the final liberation which is salvation and actual engagement in liberation here and now condition each other: the liberty lived now is a real sign of the hope of the final liberty, which Christians should not hide when, with all men of good will, they work in various sectors and on different levels for the amelioration of the conditions of life today.

The liberty for which Christ has freed and sent us is a reality of the *new creation*. It is therefore proper that in this aspect it should be incarnate and situated in human history. The world in which Christians are united with other men and women for the work of liberation in economic, cultural, social, political and international fields should make clear the totality of the liberty in which they believe and to which they are consecrated. We can hope in a truly liberating action even in the economico-political sphere only because Christ offers us a liberty which transcends such a sphere. On the other hand, where political and economic realities and the fight for their transformation assume an exclusive value, the continuous aggravation of conflicts and of individual and collective egoisms will be inevitable, because there man will always be treated as an object and all the organizations, administrations, bureaucracies and various structures become 'means of objectivization', that is, they become ideologies which express and reinforce the tendency to retain man as an object.[8] True creative and redemptive liberty is possible only in as far as people believe that they can transcend economic dimensions and live a more ample liberty.

Nevertheless Christians must humbly recognize that often, in the past, they believed that they could disregard liberty in the economic and political fields in order to enjoy the one proper to contemplation or to spiritual, intellectual or cultural activities; and thus they were mistaken, because liberty does not admit of limitation. However, to come back to the discussion, man must be freed from his being conditioned as mere object even in the economico-political sphere. Man must be recognized everywhere as the centre of liberty; and he can live such an attribute only if he is engaged in communicating it to all others on every level, using his capacities in the highest degree possible. On the one hand the Church must constitute a prophetic and critical voice in opposition to those who put their confidence exclusively in economic reconstruction, that is, those who put their exclusive confidence in the liberation from conditioning elements of an economic nature which repress the exercise of human responsibility and co-responsibility. On the other hand we must never forget that the world of today will judge us according to the fruit that our faith bears in our commitment to liberty in the decisive sectors of the well-being, autonomy and future of humanity. 'Evangelization will therefore depend on the measure in which the Church, as seen by her members and society, proves to be an institution which does not obstruct individual liberty, but rather promotes it in her internal sphere and helps to defend and conserve it in the social sphere.'[9] We have no chance of proclaiming the Word incarnate as Liberator and Saviour if we ignore the incarnation of liberty in the various spheres of life.

In the history of salvation the concepts of liberty, liberation, justice, peace and reconciliation are united. This universal vision should constitute a characteristic mark of the commitment of Christians to the cause of liberty. Not only their motivation, but their concrete contribution itself should show with absolute clarity that one cannot hope for liberty nor act for liberation if one does not see peace and reconciliation as gifts that should be received with that sort of gratitude which renders us ready to be peaceful men, builders of peace and messengers of reconciliation. This criterion also determines the possibilities and modalities of co-operation between Christians and adherents of ideologies which emphasize the conflict unilaterally and approve of, if not directly favour, hatred between classes or nations.

In order to be a sacrament, a visible and effective sign of liberation, the Church must discern the signs of the times. In fact, 'the whole of humanity lives a sort of gigantic exodus: it passes from one era to another'.[10] It is therefore important to educate all the faithful to live the profound biblical spirituality of the exodus and the paschal mysteries. They should not cling to the past, but, grateful for the past and the promises contained in it, should prepare themselves for the passage to the future. Their expectation of the Lord of history should be obvious in watchfulness for the opportunities which the present hour offers for the promotion of liberty, peace and justice.

B. *The choice of the poor*

In one of the preceding chapters I have already reflected a

little on the fact that the Church herself must become more evangelical. She must be poor among the poor. What is the content of this affirmation and what does it indicate?

The Church of necessity addresses herself to the poor. And even when she evangelizes the powerful and the rich, it is to make them conscious of their misery unless they are willing to be converted to the poor, so that the poor may really feel themselves blessed in the kingdom of Christ. The central content of the message and testimony of the Church should therefore be the first beatitude, which includes all the others: blessed are those who, through the Holy Spirit, are humble and poor, because the kingdom of heaven is theirs. If men accept the good news of Christ the Servant, then they no longer exploit others, but consider them as brothers and sisters.[11] Obviously, this does not exclude the fact that on certain occasions the first attention could be given to the directing *élite*, especially when only they can open for us the door to evangelize the masses. It is in this manner that the Church acted in the past, especially among the Germanic and Celtic tribes. There, in fact, the people found no difficulty in following the prince who had himself accepted the good news and baptism. While, however, she gives attention to the *élite*, the Church should not lose sight of her aim: to educate the best among them with the gospel and make them servants of all, renouncing their unjust privileges which do harm to fraternity and the rights of others.

In this way, the option of the Church in favour of the poor does not become a partisan choice, because it aims at converting all to evangelical poverty, simplicity and justice. And if the Church knows how to convert those who have riches, power and knowledge to the one God, the Father and Redeemer of all, she will also convert them to the poor, the discriminated against and left on the fringe. She must however witness and preach at the same time to the poor themselves their own beatitude, in order that they should not consciously or unconsciously pursue the kind of aims of the non-converted rich and powerful.

The evangelization of the poor in the spirit of the first beatitude forbids the Church from entering into any kind of alliance with the rich and powerful, an alliance which may arouse suspicion of sacralizing an unjust *status quo*. She should, however, co-operate with whoever is in authority, and carefully avoid opting for systematic anticonformism in her confrontations with any actual structure. This co-operation will consist chiefly in always witnessing to the gospel which is preached to the poor, with that integrity which includes and promotes social justice and peace.

The Church will not accept an alliance which is in support of the *status quo* even if that would be to obtain the help of the rich, no matter how noble the scope for which this is intended. This does not mean that she should refuse or despise alms given by the rich; but these cannot be accepted in exchange for coming to terms with or recognizing an unjust situation. Besides, one must not forget that generally it is not the very rich who support the works of the Church, but the many who have just a little more than is necessary who share generously this little with those poorer than themselves.

If the choice to help the poor is to be faithful to the evangelizing mission, it must not end in work of a supplementary sort or with economic help. Charitable work and social help will always be necessary because there will never be a perfect political or social system. Moreover, the Church will, in that way, be contributing a human and evangelical element which distributive justice alone will never be able to offer. But having said this, I would like to underline that the choice of the poor is a prophetic option in favour of social justice. 'To limit oneself to marginal actions, when it is possible to change situations radically, means to betray both love for man and love for God.'[12]

Authentic evangelization is in itself humanization and education for fraternity and true justice.[13] The Church should follow the example of the great prophets and Christ, *the* Prophet, who have on every occasion explicitly drawn conclusions from faith in one God and in the alliance; a faith which translates itself into justice, peace and fraternity, a faith which is anxious that the poor, migrant workers, strangers, people on the fringe of society and those discriminated against should be respectful. Social doctrine and pedagogy which prepare this faith are integral parts of evangelization, because it is impossible to be converted in the Holy Spirit to the gospel of the one

God, Creator and Redeemer without an authentic conversion to justice, peace and reconciliation which are inseparable parts of this gospel.

Evangelization of the poor and the choice of them can sometimes involve the Church in the conflict between oppressed and oppressors, exploited and exploiters. It is not possible, however, for the Church to accept a spirit and method of conflict which contradict the gospel and do not consciously tend towards true reconciliation. Her presence should not worsen conflicts, but should support and strengthen a shared non-violent action that favours justice and universal liberty. If we want to use the word 'conflict' we should clearly explain its meaning so as to determine it precisely, in opposition to Marxist and other types of ideology which easily justify violence and hatred. Ours is a real and involved fight which will always include our own continuous conversion and social reform without leading to new forms of injustice and oppression, and which will be inspired by faith in the one God the Creator, and in Christ the Redeemer, and therefore, will always be inspired by a healing love of all, including even those whom we must oppose and strip of their unjust position.

Christians who believe they must unite their evangelical struggle to that of men inspired by other ideologies must be spiritually prepared not only to discern, but also to give clear witness to their faith, which disapproves ideologies and methods that do not intend universal reconciliation; otherwise they will not be able to display their stimulating function, but will inevitably be influenced by those who should have been led to a more complete awareness of the right scale of values.

When we humbly accept the Marxist contestation against erroneous forms of religion — including erroneous forms of Christianity — which, in their deviation, are expressions of sin (alienation and evasion), and when we are filled with hunger and passionate thirst for the solidarity and hope of a truly just and fraternal society — not being concerned whether Marx or Mao Tse Tung or any one else also shares similar hopes — we shall be able to engage in an enduring dialogue serenely refuting all misleading and dangerous ideologies.

The mission of the Church consists above all in a constructive and thus pacific presence. In our vocabulary 'the conflict'

— even the most just and holy one — can never have the principal place. We are always aiming for the reconciliation of all in justice and mutual respect.

In the past and still today, the Church has begun many educational projects which constitute the first step for the poor to be able to arrive at an active participation in social life; she has created everywhere, especially among the most needy, a wonderful school and social help system which is part of her witnessing and evangelizing presence. But when the people, the societies or the states for whom these projects were constructed reach a stage of maturity and preparation which permits them to continue these projects by themselves, the Church would be witnessing to the first beatitude if she would voluntarily hand over what she has constructed without accepting compensation for it. This act of understanding and confidence would render the Church more free to further her mission of evangelization in new forms and relationships. In saying this I am particularly concerned about 'the third world'. I do not suggest that we should cease to help and improve those educational facilities that guarantee an integration of faith and life.

The enormous growth of the population of the world, particularly in the developing countries, the solidarity that binds the rich nations and classes in opposition to these developing nations, the danger of the exhaustion of primarily important material resources, the ecological equilibrium put at risk by air and water pollution and many other worrying phenomena necessarily impose on the human race an energetic conversion from consumerism to austere simplicity. A *third revolution* through which people may regain their interior liberty is imminent. And this will surely be the critical point for the testimony of Christians. 'Although we are actually tempted by arrogance and consumerism, we know that they are aberrations which have no room in our fundamental Christian philosophy. Even if we try to ignore them, we know the fundamental doctrines of the gospel — that the poor are blessed, the nonviolent will inherit the earth and the peace-makers are children of God. We know that contemplation and adoration are the highest possible recompense in human experience. When justice demands a better distribution of material goods, Christians, in order to meet this new demand with sympathy, have a solid vision of simplicity and contemplative joy. They are not condemned to resentment and lamentable regret. On the contrary, they can turn the more humble material levels into spiritual riches and thus discover the joy of giving and sharing that the world cannot take away.'[14] In this context the great economist Barbara Ward also says a challenging word on the meaning of the religious life of those who live poverty and simplicity in the service of the gospel, affirming that they will not be something of little importance left over from the Middle Ages, but 'the joyous people of the twenty-first century, most modern and most relevant, men and women who will be more necessary for our days.'[15] They will be indispensable witnesses inspiring lay Christians engaged in works for justice, peace and reconciliation in the age we are entering into. However, we must not wait for the moment in which economic breakdown will impose on us a most severe austerity. Christians will be witnesses of the ultimate future, if the immediate future, together with the eschatological hope, is taken as an effective motive for deepening their conversion to the beatitude foreseen for and promised to those who possess the spirit of the poor.

C. *Evangelization and political engagement*

Political theology has drawn profit from the various studies of religious and pastoral sociology which consider the interdependence between the totality of religious expressions and social, economic, cultural and political life.[16] It invites all Christians, and especially theologians and official teachers of the Church to be and to become more and more conscious of the influence exercised by the social structures on the thought and structure of religion, and vice-versa, and to become equally conscious of the influence which their taking up of a position or their inactivity exercises on the life of the *polis*.[17]

I use the term 'politics' here, not only in the particular sense of political decisions, but also in the wider sense of '*polis*': the life of a society, which includes every aspect: economic, cultural, communitarian and so on.

1. *The Church as the critical conscience of society* — The better knowledge of history today and, above all, empirical sociology and social psychology facilitate, and impose on the members of the Church, especially those who exercise a particular authority, the making of a continual critical examination of every religious structure, including those of liturgy, theological thought and the way in which the teaching authority carries out its function. The constant examination makes it possible to be sure whether a structure is a conscious response to the gospel and to the signs of the times, or whether, on the contrary, there are spurious influences that arise from negative conditionings in secular society. Above all, when the Church is not aware of these interdependences, she proceeds under the influence of a scarcely redeemed society, and does not profit from the opportunities thus found in the better parts of that society.

The Church can be the critical spirit of society, as she should always be, only if she develops a most critical conscience with regard to the influences that she herself undergoes from economic, political and cultural structures and judges with evangelical criteria. And by 'Church' I mean all the faithful, communities and ministers, but particularly the authorities and structures. Similarly, in saying 'society', I do not in the first place mean what is outside the ecclesial orbit, but Christians who are part of the secular city and should take active responsibility in it. Nevertheless we cannot forget society as such and all those who are part of it without being members of the Church. The critical word of ecclesiastical authority is directed above all to the faithful, while the complete testimony of the people of God addresses itself to the whole of humanity.

With the gospel, the Church has to preach complete conversion. This cannot be limited to the individual aspect of human existence. 'Conversion and preaching are always events of God's kingdom, and this kingdom is always a reality also for society and history. . . The preaching of repentance and conversion is not a sacralization of the existing conditions, but rather a strong call to the future, and therefore, liberation. The individual and the community must behave as penitents, walking on the road of conversion. . . Sin and redemption have social dimensions and therefore enter into the political sphere.'[18] 'The "critical" proclamation of the gospel denounces the limits, the provisory nature of objectives attained, and relativizes ideologies.'[19]

United to the prophets and Christ, the Church ceaselessly fights against idols and ideologies; she unmasks and condemns all forms of 'sacred egoism' and the law which favours only the strong maintained by the powerful.

In order to be a prophetic voice and a true liberating witness, the people of God, and especially those constituted in authority, must continuously be on the watch so that they may not become instruments of or be manipulated by any faction of society. Often, public opinion used by a group or a political power willingly denounces with force the ideologies, errors and crimes of the adversary, while enveloping in complacent silence the misdeeds and abuses, sometimes very grave, committed perhaps by friends or others more powerful. It can also happen that pressure is put on ecclesiastics to make declarations in favour of a public opinion which is based on one-sided information or even twisted facts.

For many years I have been strongly interested in the problem of the liberation of the various African nations under colonial rule. I willingly joined many other voices in condemning colonialism and racism. I saw with sympathy and perceived the positive value of the contestation of the White Fathers, who preferred to abandon their mission in Mozambique rather than justify the Portuguese presence in the concrete form it took, and saw that with such a prophetic gesture they powerfully reminded the Church of her necessary independence of the colonizing state. But in the end I asked myself why public opinion, international and ecclesial, had not reacted with the same or even greater vigour against the enormous crimes committed by a small minority of Watussi against the Bahutu majority in Burundi. This was a question of a premeditated massacre of at least 250,000 persons, aimed particularly at those who would have become the political élite in a future in which the Bahutus would no longer be deprived of their lawful rights in their own country. And yet the world and the Church remained silent or in any case seemed to use excessive care when a word was ssaid against this massive genocide and the unimaginable anguish that it brought. Again we can only be puzzled by the fact that when the oppressed Bahutus in Rwanda rebelled and killed some thousands of Watussi, the world seemed very much alarmed, despite the fact that after their rebellion the Bahutus did not deprive their former oppressors of their political rights.

Prophetic denunciation demands knowledge of the situation and discernment. The representatives of the Church in particular should not speak without reliable information and without having reflected well on the possible consequences of their words. The play, *The Vicar*, by Hochhuth, harshly accused Pius XII of not having denounced the massacre of the Jews with prophetic vigour. It is however proved how concerned the Pope was at heart about the lot of the persecuted. The most courageous denunciation made at that time by the Dutch Episcopate provoked the fury of the Nazi criminals and increased the persecution in Holland. 'The Dutch Cardinal De Jong protested against the persecution of the Jews and thus caused new victims. Sometimes man finds no escape from a situation in which he has no other choice but to "choose" his victims. Would to God that were not true.'[20] In the dark moments of uncontrollable oppression in which the Church cannot openly contest, she must continue to contest by way of constructive witnessing. That is to say, her behaviour in such circumstances should be such that it will help men of good will to resist idols and ideologies. A sober and positive teaching will give sufficient light to all those who truly want to see and who are sincerely ready to listen. She should never fail to promote nonviolent resistance.

2. *The political vocation* — The importance which the political field assumes in the life of people is a motive for considering the political vocation as one of the most significant. It is surely a difficult vocation which demands an adequate professional preparation and a particular charism of *parrhesia* (boldness and sincerity), strength of character and purity of motives.

In an epoch in which the Church is particularly aware that she must be the critical conscience also of public life, and above all in an epoch in which there are so many contesting voices, it will not be difficult for politicians to find tranquillizing voices by which to direct their examination of conscience. Today the same society offers clamorous cases of sharp examination and judgement: think back to the 'Watergate' affair. At the present moment which is difficult in so many ways, the critical voice of the Church should nevertheless not be raised in such a way as to discourage good men from entering the political field. On the contrary, conscientious awareness of the political life should lead the best men and women to ask themselves whether perhaps they do have this special vocation, and help them in the necessary moral and professional preparation. And even when criticism is inevitable it should never eliminate sentiments of respect and recognition of good will.

We cannot however close our eyes to the fact that many decisions taken and promulgated by governments and parliaments consider a situation as cut and dried. Therefore, the narrow concept of a Catholicism which plays all its cards in the political field considered in the most strict sense has to be avoided. In fact, the authentic renewal of the Church, the effective education of all Christians in a sense of responsibility, professional morals, intelligent and competent participation in the process of the formation of public opinion will be felt more in the political arena than a specific strategy and ability. For example, everybody knows that the stability of marriage, Christtian or non-Christian, and the protection of the child still in the mother's womb, do not depend exclusively nor primarily on political decisions. Therefore if the Chruch wants to be what she should be, she cannot pay attention only to political analysis nor pretend that the laws correspond *sic et simpliciter* to her own moral code. She has, much more, to sharpen consciences and indicate constructive ways of thought and action. She should educate the faithful to be able to participate in the forming of healthy public opinion and the finding of courageous initiatives.

3. *The various roles in the Church* — The famous Protestant moralist Paul Ramsey[21] accused a part of the authorities and groups of the Ecumenical Council of Churches of indulging in a new clericalism, that is to say, of claiming for themselves decisions and judgements in matters where they widely lack true competence. At the same time it is interesting to note

the favourable judgement which the same author made of the way in which the Second Vatican Council and the encyclical letters, *Pacem in terris* of John XXIII and *Populorum progressio* of Paul VI, express themselves in matters of social and political ethics. In these documents Ramsey noted a style which permits one to have a glimpse of a new conscience in relation to the limits of competence.

The Church can, effectively, be a critical conscience in society only if she accepts herself as a choir in which each singer has his specific role. Everyone should perceive the limits of his charism and knowledge.

The ecclesial magisterium — pope and bishops — and, under its authority, theologians, must, in the social and political field, put the accent on the dynamism of faith towards responsibility. Both will be contributing in the most valuable way if they educate all the faithful to work out a synthesis between faith and life, between dogma and morals and to be on the lookout for the signs of the times. It is one thing to communicate the great visions of the prophets and the gospel, it is another to put the prophetic word in a concrete situation: they must be mindful of the limits of their human formation; prudence advises them to accept the advice of those in a position to give it. Without this dialogue which unites the best of human experience in shared reflection, the magisterium can never represent a prophetic voice in the present world whose complexity is such that it cannot be compared to the one in which the prophets of Israel worked.

The Pontifical Commission for Justice and Peace is a sign of this awareness. It develops and keeps contact with numerous experts of various disciplines and of diverse nations and cultures, expressing itself with that *parrhesia* which is a proof of its passionate love for justice and peace, but also with that prudent discretion implied in the knowledge of the complexity of social and political phenomena. Paul Ramsey praised particularly the style used by Paul VI to address his appeal for peace to the world in the full awareness of the limits of his competence.[22] If the official representatives of the Church think that they must say something on political questions, they should not forget the many errors committed in the past when, seduced by false messianism or triumphalism, churchmen wanted to judge or impose choices of a political character obviously going beyond their own competence.

One would be demanding too much from the popes and the bishops if one were to put them under pressure to express approval and/or eventual condemnation on all the major political issues. While we must greatly appreciate the prophetic spirit present in the Church we have no right to presume that every pope or bishop automatically has the prophetic charism for every sector of social and political life. We must all listen to the prophetic voices, and every part of the Church — magisterium, theologians, priests, educators — should prepare the faithful to recognize the authentic prophets. Thus I go back once more to stress the primary importance of education in discernment.

4. *The pluralism of political choice* — In consideration of the importance proper to each political decision and of the co-responsibility pertaining to all Christians in modern society, each one must regard his political choice as a very fundamental decision of conscience. Therefore each one should seriously acquire information on the meaning of political life, carefully analyse the situation and rigorously examine the motives that lead to a particular choice. Christians can never associate themselves with the 'sacred egoisms' of groups and social classes, but must always consider first the common good, and only in this perspective can they also consider the legitimate interests of their groups or social classes. Since political situations are complex and the confrontations between various legitimate interests uncertain, it is not surprising that Christians do not always arrive at the same option. 'The same Christian faith can lead to diverse decisions'.[22] The Second Vatican Council also stressed very much the autonomy of the earthly reality and, in the first place, the political sphere. It does not therefore belong to ecclesiastical authority to deputize for the faithful in the electoral choice.

All the same, when there are critical moments in the history of a people and there arises a vigorous hostile movement against religion and/or against justice and peace, whereby the more fundamental values of conscience are disturbed, it should not be surprising that the bishops invite Christians to be united in the defence of the basic and inalienable rights of human beings. This cannot however be in any way considered as the common situation. Let us rather look at the affirmation of the Council: 'Let the layman not imagine that his pastors are always such experts that to every problem which arises, however complicated, they can readily give him a concrete solution, or even that such is their mission. Rather, enlightened by Christian wisdom and giving close attention to the teaching authority of the Church, let the layman take on his own distinctive role' (*Gaudium et spes*, 43). Most especially in this moment of history it is necessary that all citizens should be involved in providing better solutions to the most urgent problems. This common commitment and search would surely give the best results and often lead to similar proposals that would allow of solidary action.

However, it is difficult to imagine a sincere research which is deprived of the free manifestation of various points of view. 'An effective plurality of opinion is an integral part of the common good.'[24] Authentic Christians will try to acquire wisdom in politics and politics according to faith. This will create a unity of hearts and minds, and a readiness for constructive dialogue, which never loses its fecundity even in disagreements and clashes. The Second Vatican Council offers a valuable orientation towards ways of dealing with these tensions which can be verified among Christians who are equally sincere in their search. 'Often enough the Christian view of things will itself suggest some specific solution in certain circumstances. Yet it happens rather frequently, and legitimately so, that with equal sincerity some of the faithful will disagree with others on a given matter. Even against the intentions of their proponents, however, solutions proposed on one side or another may be easily confused by many people with the gospel message. Hence it is necessary for people to remember that no one is allowed in such situation to appropriate the Church's authority for his opinion. People should always try to enlighten one another through honest discussion, preserving mutual charity and caring above all for the common good' (*Gaudium et spes*, 43).

It is not only bishops and priests, but also the faithful engaged in politics, who must always remember the affirmation made by Mahatma Gandhi: in concrete solutions one cannot be infallible. It is therefore necessary that one should be ready for the best possible compromise in the search.[25] For political action it will be indispensable to elaborate a theology of compromise which takes into account the gradualness of social renewal and individual conversion and the complexity of the political situation. Dogmatism which judges politics with static criteria and which often associates itself with perfectionism, can become one of the worst enemies of the common good and social peace. In the moral sense one can, however, speak of an accepted responsibility, and propose compromise only when one searches sincerely for the best possible step, being always ready to go beyond it, in the direction of a still more just and human society.

As the confrontation of choices made with sincerity and the clash between legitimate interests, or, sometimes, egoisms generate dangerous tensions, the Church must fulfil her role as sacrament of reconciliation. She must be the place where Christians meet one another in the presence of God, to confirm in one another the will to look for the common good together for the honour of the one and only Father, and mutually to respect each other in this search. 'Perhaps, the best way may be for those responsible for the Church to multiply contacts with people of every opinion, of every current so as to show their unwillingness to be imprisoned by any of them, but to be independent of all. This would not mean indifference or lack of sincerity, but would mean that they could truly bear witness to Jesus Christ.'[26]

D. *Evangelization and fighting against unjust manipulation*

God has confided the whole of creation to man and woman. Even its biological and psychological heritage is confided to their responsible liberty. Scientific and technical progress has greatly increased their real capacity in this domain. But this becomes progress in liberty if they grow in moral liberty, in the liberty of the children of God. In every sector of life — especially in medical therapy, in psychotherapy, and with the new means of social communication — man and woman have new means of liberating themselves from unfavourable conditioning of different kinds. For example, they liberate themselves from what is caused in the psychological sphere, in the depths of the soul, when previous repressions are brought to full consciousness. Nevertheless, the use of these modern instruments can become a possible manipulation of the person when they fall into the hands of people who are not oriented towards authentic liberty. If egoism and greed, hunger and thirst for consumption reign, the entire domination of nature, of human resources and of the worker-producers themselves become manipulated, while man and woman make themselves slaves to these new conditioning elements which constitute the investment or the concrete incarnation of sin as a whole.

People today are often attracted by this new form of fideistic blindness and thus submit themselves to the ultimate pseudo-discoveries of a superficially popularized science which ignores the genuine scientific spirit, to which consciousness of the tentative nature and the limits of a particular branch of science are never foreign, while it is inevitably open to new progress and to a much wider synthesis embracing all the sciences and theories in the light of the total good of persons. If the Church lives the gospel and knows how to communicate the good news she will liberate the believers from superficiality and concupiscence and arrogance and the desire to manipulate others.

Together with disordered concupiscence, the worst enemies of human freedom are superficiality, dissipation and distraction, either of the individual or of the group. The Church on the other hand educates people in contemplation, so that they may find their *Sabbath*, their rest in the Lord Emmanuel, and be vigilant for the coming of the Lord in a continuous reflection on the events of life in the light of the gospel. Only in this way, being mindful of his peace, can a person acquire and preserve interior liberty; a condition which is indispensable for Christian involvement in the liberation of humanity at all levels and in all the sectors of life.

The great power of the means of social communication can be an instrument of mutual dialogue and balanced information, but can also unfortunately become a means of massive manipulation. By educating believers in discernment, in a sense of responsibility and in a healthy asceticism, the Church protects them from sensationalism. Christians should be in this field of social communication with serenity, with a lucid and rigorous analysis and with that sort of liberty in dialogue which will help all to listen attentively and liberate both the manipulators and the manipulated. The ecclesial community will be a sacrament of liberty and continuous liberation if it creates within itself a climate of passionate search for the truth and for the best solutions to new problems, in a spirit of discernment which does not confuse doctrines that are only opinions, and not even traditional formulations with the substance of the *depositum fidei*. To the extent to which the Church has educated each of her members in this dialogue— which is liberating, serene and conducted in an atmosphere of contemplation and engagement that leads to the practice of the truth discovered she will be able to offer a true model to secular society so as to help it use the means of social communication and all the other instruments in its power to dominate natural forces in a genuine spirit of liberty. When the Church recognizes and humbly admits her errors in this field, she communicates to all the very necessary awareness that sinful man and woman must be strictly vigilant in order not to let themselves be manipulated by the ideologies of the tribe and of the market place.

NOTES

1 Cf. B. Ward. *A New Creation? Reflections on the Environmental Issue*, Rome, 1973, pp. 18–28.
2 Cf. J. Dournes, 'Reposer le problème de l'évangélisation ou: du christianisme comme libération de l'homme', in *Spiritus* 10 (1969), pp. 158–172.
3 Synod of bishops, *Justice in the World*, Rome, 1971.
4 Cf. B. Sorge, 'Evangelizzazione e impegno politico', *Civiltà Cattolica* IV (1973) 8; *Gaudium et spes*, 42–45.
5 Spanish Bishops' Conference, *The Church and the Political Community*, 24. The document is cited according to the translation of *Presenza*, Quaderni di Spiritualità, Rocca di Papa, 8 (1972), pp. 53–54.
6 Cf. B. Sorge, *op. cit.*, p. 13.
7 Cf. R. Zerfass, 'Herrschaftsfreie Verkündigung', in *Diakonia* 4 (1973), pp. 350.
8 This is one of the fundamental concepts of the philosophy of Berdyaev, for whom the most profound alienation is shown in those objectivizations which derive from the lack of expression of creative liberty by man on all levels. Cf. P. Klein, *Berdyauv und die schöpferische Freiheit*, Doctoral dissertation, Accademia Alfonsiana, Rome 1974.

9 K. Lehman, 'Konflikte und Chancen in Glaubensverständnis und Verkündigung', in *Befragte Katholiken* p. 54; also K. Forster: reflecting on the German bishops' enquiry (*op. cit., p.* 10), he draws the same conclusion; Cf. also A. Schmied, 'Vermittlungen der Erlösung', in *Theologie der Gegenwart* 16 (1913), pp. 171–176; H. W. Daigler, *Heutiges Menschenrechtsbewusstsein und Kirche*, Cologne, 1973; A. Rizzi, 'Teologia della liberazione: Una Protesta e una promessa dall'America Latina', in *Rivista di Teologia Morale* 5 (1973), 17, pp. 53–85.

10 French Bishops' Conference, *Politics, Faith and the Church,* preliminary declaration.

11 Cf. G. Simon, B. Häring, *Politics of the Kingdom,* London, 1966.

12 A. Revelli, 'Evangelizzazione e scelta dei poveri', in *Note di Pastorale Giovanile* 5 '(1973), p. 36.

13 Cf. N. Goodall, *Christian Missions and Social Ferment,* London, 1964.

14 B. Ward, *A New Creation? Reflections on the Environmental Issue, pp. 67–68.*

15 *Ibid.,* p. 68.

16 Cf. B. Häring, *Introduzione alla sociologia religiosa e pastorale*, Rome, 1965, 2nd edition.

17 Cf. R. Coste, *Vangelo e politica, Bologna, 1970; G. Mattai, 'Morale Politica',* Bologna, 1971; *Presenza,* Quaderni di spiritualità 8 (1972), the whole of this number is dedicated to political engagement as an engagement of faith. A.A. V.V., *Dibattito sulla teologia politicia,* Brescia, 1972, 2nd ed.

18 J. Bommer, 'Verkündigung als geseltschaftkritischer Vorgang', in *Diakonia* 4 (1973), p. 299.

19 B. Sorge, *Evangelizzazione e impegno politico,* p. 22.

20 W. A. Luijpen, *Existential Phenomenology,* Pittsburgh, 1969, p. 223.

21 Cf. P. Ramsey, *Who Speaks for the Church?*, Nashville, 1967; *The Just War: Force and political Responsibility*, New York, 1968; C. Curran, *Politics, Medicine and Christian Ethics— A Dialogue With Paul Ramsey,* Philadelphia, 1973, pp. 11–109.

22 Cf. P. Ramsey, *Who Speaks for the Church?,* p. 53.

23 Paul VI, *Octogesima adveniens,* 50.

24 Spanish Bishops' Conference, *The Church and the Political Community,* 20.

25 Cf. J. Thekkinedath, *Love of Neighbour in Mahatma Gandhi*, Bangalore, 1972; Doctrinal dissertation presented at Accademia Alfonsiana.

26 French Bishops' Conference, *Politics, Faith and the Church,* p. 5, 3.

4

Evangelization in the age of exodus

1. *The situation*

Humanity today and in the immediate future lives a great exodus allegorically similar to the one of Israel from Egypt. We live a transition from one era to another. Of this we know some features but not the image of the whole. It is an exodus of the centres of influence which pass from the first and second worlds to the third world, from old Europe and North America to Asia, Africa and Latin America, where the population, particularly young, continually increases, while, on the contrary, that of Europe and America progressively gets old. This fact creates grave tensions between old and young in the continents that have up to now dominated the earth. To use an image we could say that today St Peter would most probably not choose Antioch nor Rome and not even New York as his see, but one of the big cities recently constituted world centres: Lagos, or Peking, or Tokyo, and the possibilities would be very numerous. The exodus also exists within what I have called the first and second worlds themselves. We shall be caught in a 'third revolution' which will radically shake both the capitalist and the communist worlds.

The presence of Marxist communism has been a characteristic note of our century. But while communism still tries to present itself as a great political and economic power, as a movement it is already dead, since the quasi-religious faith in its doctrines and ideology are rapidly being extinguished among the young.

If the Church wants to be the leaven in the loaf of human history, she must be fully aware of and prepare herself for this gigantic exodus which has already started but is far from completion, though on the other hand it is accelerating its rhythm. If the ecclesial community wants to walk with the Lord of history it must orient itself towards the new centres of population and influence, yet without ignoring the evangelization of the old.

In this exodus, there is a great hope which is the encounter between Christianity and deeply religious character of Africans and the great oriental contemplative religions and moral cultures — Confucianism for example, or the new forms of Buddhism which look for a synthesis between detachment and presence, between moral-social religion and contemplation. The encounter with the great contemplative religions such as Buddhism, Hinduism and some parts of Islam could perhaps be of even greater importance. The Church will be preparing herself better for these encounters and for the evangelization of the continents indicated if she knows how to present herself not only as a moral teacher with a social gospel, but with that deep faith which assures the growth of contemplation and produces genuinely evangelical morals.

In the first and second worlds, the Church has begun to realize fully that the age of the *Corpus Christianum* is over. Her position is now again that of a *diaspora* in a world whose pluralism of ideologies and scales of values is sometimes distressing. In the third world she will meet not only with the ancient traditions of these peoples, but with cultures which are developing and are full of tensions caused by the encounter with western mentality and the influence of capitalism, Marxism, the sense of modernity and, finally, of the gospel which however is still often clothed in a very occidental form.

2. *The evangelizing response to this different world*

The question put to the Church, which will always be put to her, is: does she truly walk with the whole human race in such a way as to testify that she accompanies the Lord of history and to give a serene orientation to humanity in this epoch of a gigantic exodus?

All that I have said on pluralism in the ecclesial sphere is proposed here with new dimensions in the hope of a new Pentecost, but is also a cause of anxiety and of a complex neurosis of insecurity. Thus the Christian people should be so deeply united in a single faith and in such an expectation and watchfulness for the Lord who comes and will come to remain forever, as to become a sacrament of unity in the many difficulties connected with this exodus of which we speak.

The behavioural sciences — cultural sociology, matrimonial and family sociology, the sociology of religion — have shown the interdependence existing at the core of every culture and of every era. Religion cannot continue to be vital and effective if it refuses to incarnate itself in a new way in the whole project of actual cultures, accepting the state of exodus and the possibilities of meeting and promoting new syntheses. The pedagogy of faith and, to a greater degree, that of morals must learn from the pedagogy of development which affirms the impossibility of imposing the same system of controls or of liberty on a child, an adolescent and an adult, and rather upholds the necessity of gradual development. But furthermore, to acquire the experience and to receive the help of modern sciences, the Church must learn, probably with pain and tensions, a new style to fit her mission: to be a ray of hope and a sure and humble guide in this new age.

It is absolutely impossible in a modest book like this one to offer theoretical solutions or complete practical systems for dealing with the problems that have been set out. I repeat, however, that if the Church would live her existence in a special watchfulness for the signs of the times, she would pay greater attention to major lines of orientation and be less obsessed with meticulous applications. This means she would live with greater conviction the necessary detachment for the sake of a new presence and incarnation. In a word, she would give particular attention to discernment, to the evangelical spirit of poverty and contemplation, this however, in such a way as to respond to the situation of exodus and of journeying towards a new future, to be a stronger witness of the hope of the absolute future.

I should like to remind the reader that what I present on the following pages is on the level of reflection: I do not intend to suggest to priests and faithful immediate applications, but I want humbly and sincerely to contribute to ecclesial thinking on various problems. Where pastoral themes in general and new methods arise, it should never be forgotten that the Church has a hierarchical structure, without which unity and peace could not be guaranteed; especially in the more difficult moments which demand the giving of a solid and unifying response to deep transformations and the relevant changes of the centres of influence. That does not prevent those who know well the major directives given by the Second Vatican Council and the central government of the Church, the Pope and the Synod of Bishops, from making decisions in the field left to free initiative; the one confided to the individual bishop as distinct from those reserved to Bishops' Conferences or to the successor of Peter. An attentive reader will not have difficulty in deducing from the formulation itself what my thought and intention are.

In this context I want only to touch on a few subjects which I have studied and discussed often during the past few years, especially in Africa. I shall not enter into casuistry about the ultimate applications and consequences, because this would be precisely to contradict the more obvious demands of an answer to this world which is in full transformation. At least for Africa the three most interesting and most discussed problems are: a) *polygamy,* b) *the indissolubility of a sterile marriage,* especially in cultures which up to now have always made fertility the indispensable condition for the finalization of the marriage contract, and c) *the manner in which the marriage alliance comes gradually into being.* The problem of private and common property should also be mentioned, but there the Church has already come to grasp the problems of pluralism.

A. *Polygamy*[1]

1. *The complexity of the problem* — The old world, Europe and North America, is heading speedily towards massive successive polygamy and successive polyandry, that is, of men and women who have two, three or more wives and husbands respectively, using divorce to attain such ends, while the earlier spouses are still alive. Furthermore, whereas in nearly all cultures of the past sexuality was completely put under the control of social norms, today we are witnessing the emancipation of great masses of people, both adolescents and adults, who live their own sex life free from any external interference. This state of affairs brings ever greater problems to the Church,

who must search for solutions in full awareness of the new situation and of the opportunities which are connected with it. The Church must resist disastrous and disintegrating tendencies and, at the same time, remain present with the compassion of Christ among all those involved in these new currents coming from the changing conditions of life. We can hope that the *third revolution*, imposing a more simple life, will succeed in reversing this dangerous tendency towards a dissolved family and social life.

We must never lose sight of this situation of the old world, which still influences the new, when we confront problems such as the polygamy existing in large regions of Africa and in some parts of Asia.

The problem of African polygamy is even suitable for illustrating the complexity of the present age of transition. It has been put afresh in a new form and with new emotions after decolonization, which has been in its turn followed by a new self-comprehension and self-awareness in the African cultures, and after the big opening given by the Second Vatican Council to cultures different from those of Europe. The problem of polygamy is confronted by the African Churches as a whole and not only by Catholics. In this confrontation they keep in due consideration the old traditions which are often still alive, and the African revival of today, but also a mature awareness of the traditional theses of the Church and of the new dynamism of cultural transformation. The local ecclesial communites and the more attentive and sensitive theologians have re-examined the question with a re-reading of scripture, meditating on the divine pedagogy of the Old Testament, in the light of recent anthropological and social sciences. It is therefore not a question of an abstract discussion. Whoever wants to propose or suggest solutions which can be put into practice must take into account all the complexity of the situation, not overlooking any element or facet.

2. *The traditional solution* — When the Christian Churches began their evangelization in Asia and Africa they encountered polygamy; and they judged it with the only canon they knew: the monogamy of the *Corpus Christianum*. Practically everywhere, the missionaries showed a deep contempt for

polygamy which they variously defined as 'adultery', 'fornication', 'concubinage' and so on. For them there was no doubt about the state of sin in which the polygamist was living. They were not even in a position, nor did they even care, to imagine the diverse social and cultural signification which polygamy had in the different tribes and they did not take into account that it was found practically all over Africa.

Today we know that about eighty per cent of the tribes south of the Sahara have polygamy as their preferred system. This means that, in general, the monogamist is by no means considered as being better, but is rather a potential polygamist who regrets the fact that he has not yet succeeded. There remains the other twenty per cent of tribes in which monogamy is equally or more esteemed than polygamy. One should also not forget that Africans make a clear distinction between polygamy socially approved and irregular or disapproved polygamy. Here we are concerned with only that form of polygamy which is socially approved. In the Africa of today as in that of the past, polyandry is practically unknown.

The solution of the Catholic, Anglican and Protestant missionaries was arrogant and firm: whoever wanted to be baptized had to rebuild his family with a monogamous marriage. This meant that the polygamous husband who wanted baptism had to send away his wives, keeping only one. In some areas the missionaries, Catholic or other, showed much understanding of the woman who was living in a polygamous marriage, because it was more easily understood that the situation in which she was living did not depend on her will. All the same, according to the norm, only the first wife was baptized and only if she disapproved of the polygamous situation of her husband. The missionaries praised very much the polygamous husband who dismissed and sent away the mothers of his children in order to become a Christian.

Certainly, the missionaries did not lack compassion towards all those who were involved and especially towards the poor woman who had been sent away and the children deprived of their mother, because in patriarchal cultures the father and his clan must keep the children even if the mother has been sent away. Among the missionaries there were also some who found great difficulty in imposing such measures in the name of the principal motive of monogamy, the equal dignity of man and woman: in fact the rigid pastoral solution was imposing heavy burdens and much misery on the shoulders of the woman.[2]

3. *The new approach* — The study of anthropology and biblical renewal which pays much attention to the pedagogy used by God in his dealings with the patriarchs, who were all polygamists, have provoked a change of mentality among nearly all the indigenous African priests and the missionaries themselves of all the Churches. Today the customary polygamist who often lives in a wonderful harmony is no longer held in contempt. So far as I have been able to read in the numerous publications, most of them cyclostyled, and also from what I have heard during my visits to more than twenty African countries, in practically all the missions both men and women of customary polygamous socially approved marriages are admitted to the catechumenate and are somehow counted among the members of the Church. The proof of it is the fact that they do receive public Christian burial and prayers. Divorce (or sending away) of the second wife is not encouraged but rather discouraged, because it is realized that the scriptural statements against divorce included also this type,[3] and especially because after decades of experience, the consequences, are considered.[4] To send away the second wife and the others following her disturbs social peace and harmony and causes great disorders in public morality, because these women, completely unrooted, become easy victims of prostitution, thus spreading a hitherto unknown phenomenon.[5] One can calmly affirm that in some areas the pure and sudden abolition of socially controlled polygamy would amount to a cultural choice which favours the institution of prostitution.

One of the reasons for African polygamy is the appreciation of the corporal virginity of the girl who is to be married: it is, therefore, supposed that a woman should be given in marriage as soon as she has reached sexual maturity. On the other hand a much superior age is expected of the man. He must give proof that he is able to support a family economically. In some regions it can also be that there is a numerical difference between men and women, but this is not so often a main cause like that of the age difference between the spouses. Generalizing a bit, we can say that where polygamy is the preferred system, there one finds a proportion of a hundred and fifty married women to every hundred men. However, in spite of this almost every man has the opportunity to marry.

Many studies have shown with precision how polygamy stands in relation to various cultural, social, economic and other factors. Thus to change suddenly one of the aspects while all the others remain unchanged can lead to great disruptions.

The Christian Churches find themselves before a great problem which very much influences evangelization: how can they estimate the moral value of polygamy in the concrete situation? I think it is very important to make a clear distinction between two questions which though interdependent are very different: (i) the invitation in the name of the gospel to divorce the second and successive wives or the imposition of this divorce as a *sine qua non* of baptism; (ii) the permission or the prohibition of Christians' contracting a polygamous marriage. I shall try to answer these two questions.

i) As I have already said, there is more and more a tendency not to desire that a polygamous family which lives in harmony and with social honour be dissolved in the name of the gospel, because this brings grave damage to all involved and introduces a painful incentive or tendency to arbitrary divorce in some societies where marriage was very stable. The sending away of the second wife without any fault of hers constitutes, for the conscience of the Africans, a grave breaking of the alliance, thus a sin against fidelity, and upsets the peace between families and clans. They ask themselves whether the God of the Christians who imposes such a break could be a faithful God and good Father of all.

From these reflections is derived the solution, more and more commonly accepted, of accepting the polygamist — husband and wives — to the catechumenate, but making this catechumenate last till the death of all the wives but one or till the cessation of conjugal relations. The pastors assure these non-baptized persons that salvation comes from faith and good will, and that since they lack neither they should have no fear in regard to eternal life: that they will be saved even without baptism.[6]

This practice is surely a step forward in the history of the missions but does not seem satisfactory. In fact, I do not see how on the one hand one can fully recognize the good will of those concerned and promise them salvation through faith while at the same time refusing them the sacraments of faith. The sacramental life of the Church should communicate a message identical to the message of evangelization, that is, make visible that the Lord brings peace to all men of good will.[7] The Africans have a particularly deep intuition of the synthesis between faith and the sacraments.

Many of those who follow the practice of admitting the honest polygamists to perpetual catechumenate are convinced of the arguments given above; however, they refuse to baptize only because they want to observe the actual discipline of the Church as long as the teaching authority does not authorize a subsequent step. This in fact seems to me to be a truly convincing motive. On the other hand, it imposes on the ecclesiastical authorities the duty to reflect seriously on the problem of the credibility of the sacramental practice, because we must absolutely avoid devaluing the importance of the sacraments especially in Africa and in the other cultures which have a very acute sense of the visible signs of salvation.

I have often heard the argument against baptism which holds that the Africans would not know the distinction between the two problems: a) baptizing the polygamous family which was found as such by the gospel, and b) permitting Christians to enter into polygamous marriage. I have often had discussions with African lay people of different social classes on this subject. They feel offended by the hypothesis, and hold that they are quite in a position to distinguish the two problems, but that, if the priests are intelligent, they could help the simple and less intelligent among the laity in making this distinction. With this solution it is clear that baptism would not be given to someone who was already a catechumen when he celebrated a polygamous marriage. In fact, one of the strong motives in favour of the baptism of polygamists is in the fact that they were married when they did not yet know the will of Christ and the ecclesiastical discipline regarding polygamy.

In the missions of the various Christian confessions I have noted many cases in which the distinctions have been made,

140

and all understood them. For example baptism is given to the first wife with the reasoning that in no part of the world is the first legitimate wife excluded from the sacraments even when the husband entertains sexual relations with other women; baptism is sometimes also given in non-Catholic Churches to the other successive wives when it is evident that their condition does not derive from a free choice but rather is the lack of any possibility to act otherwise.

Where baptism of the entire polygamous family found as such by the gospel or faith is proposed as a solution, major distinctions are necessary. What is in discussion here is however only the case of socially controlled and approved polygamy, and not the excesses of the super-rich whose *harem* can certainly not be called a 'family'. A further limitation, moreover, is presented by the pursuing of stability as a better good for those involved and for the entire society. Thus we can speak of *minus malum* or of maximum good *hic et nunc* possible.

Adrian Hastings clearly proposes that the whole polygamous family be admitted to baptism and the other sacraments under determined conditions. 'A suitably disposed polygamist can in some circumstances be baptized, together with his wives and children, while fully continuing in his polygamous marriage. If this is done, they should also be admitted to Communion'.[8] A Cameroon priest, E. N. Kofon, who has pastoral experience, has made, at the conclusion of a doctoral dissertation, a more modest proposal, but only for the particular culture of the Bafut, and in view of a compromise: to admit the family to the sacraments but on condition that the man does all his best to avoid 'polysex'; in other words after the baptism, the man should normally have conjugal relations with only one wife; however there should be a certain tolerance or allowing of *epikeia*, for example, when it is in order to avoid greater disorders such as infidelity of the other wives or great unhappiness when a wife cannot again have children.

ii) The second question is quite a different one. It is concerned with whether the Church can tolerate polygamy as a type of marriage for Christians and catechumens or not.

As far as I know, generally, there is no inclination in the diverse Churches to accept that their faithful contract such a marriage. The Catholic Church considers monogamy not only as an ideal, but as normative, and believes that she must promote its development with all energy. Adrian Hastings, however, expresses a modified opinion which finds approbation in various local churches: even if the Church cannot and should not permit that one member celebrate a second marriage, she should show a pastoral understanding at least in cases in which the collective conscience pushes towards this decision, or at least approves it.[9]

It is principally a question of the polygamy which in the Old Testament was obligatory under heavy sanction: the *levirate*. In the patriarchal, patrilineal and patrilocal tribes the woman contracts not only marriage with one man, but also an alliance with his clan. She brings, as her great patrimony, her fecundity, and must always remain in the clan, even after the death of her husband. In this last case a member of the 'family' is obliged to marry her even if he himself is already married; thus, as in Israel, in many African cultures leviratic marriage, which in the final analysis is a form of polygamy, is considered a sacred duty. Another practice very diffused, which strictly follows Abraham our father in the faith, obliges the man to take a second wife if the first, after a certain time, does not show herself fertile. In a number of cases, it is the first wife herself who, with her own family, pushes her husband to this and prepares the dowry for the girl chosen, whose child will then be also her child.

In any case, among the greater part of the Bantu tribes an infertile marriage is dissolved even against the will of the spouses, because both clans want to demonstrate that the curse of sterility does not come from their own member. All things being taken into consideration the solution of Abraham is more humane than that of most of the Bantu.

Another case which is quite frequent is that the first wife who becomes sick and can no longer carry out her work by herself insists that the husband get a companion for her, who can also help her in the work.

In the face of such situations, even Christians of the utmost good will and ardent faith find themselves in true conflicts of conscience. On the one hand they do not want to go against Church discipline; yet on the other hand they feel themselves guilty and suffer remorse for betraying a custom considered sacred and also for opposing the collective conscience. And, besides, they greatly feel the important values in the traditional norms and the collective conscience which are not those proper to the ecclesiastical law.

Therefore the situation of the woman in the regions in which the old custom still exists is particularly delicate. She is often given as second wife to a polygamist, especially in cases where it is quite impossible to enter into a monogamous marriage. An example would be: if the first marriage became sterile, the wife would be married to a man who is a father of children, and therefore already married, so that she may not be deprived of motherhood, but also to show that the fault of sterility does not come from her. Sometimes, parents feel obliged to find a husband for their daughter so as not to expose her to dangers and social dishonour; similar cases could be indicated where people act under the pressure of the collective conscience.

In such situations would it not be possible to have recourse to the traditional principle of *ignorantia invincibilis?* That is to say: despite his loyalty to the Church, the individual is not able to assimilate her law which is opposed to his conscience conditioned by the community and the difficult cultural and social situation.

Father Hillman has proposed for public discussion in the Catholic Church a more radical solution which is also proposed by other theologians in the other Churches. He suggests that a greater autonomy be given to the local Churches. As God did not change the polygamic customs in Israel, but took a long time to educate them to monogamy, so could the Church allow the local communities sufficient time to accomplish the changes necessary without imposing decisions which could seem violent to the various cultures. He puts the question in a more fundamental manner: does the Catholic Church know with certainty that monogamy is the absolute norm for all Christians, even for those of the first or second generation who live in a culture in which a moderate form of polygamy is socially approved and considered even as being superior to monogamy? If a deep knowledge of the situation proves that Christians are not able to see the value of the law of monogamy which is imposed as absolute, in so far as this law provokes difficulties of a social and personal order and obstructs evangelization, can the Church not imitate Yahweh, that is, the Old Testament divine pedagogy? In this manner one can no longer avoid a profound study of what scripture says of tradition and the doctrine of the magisterium, interpreted in full awareness of the historical context in which these arose and were formulated.

It does not seem to me that one can find in scripture a proof which obliges the Church to impose monogamy as an absolute norm on every culture and immediately on the first generation of Christians. In the Old Testament there is no negative judgement against socially approved forms of polygamy, nor is there, by the way, an explicit word from Jesus. 'Nowhere in the New Testament is there any explicit commandment forbidding polygamy'.[10] At the time of Jesus polygamy did not really constitute a big problem for Israel: it was still legitimate according to the Jewish law but was not diffused.[11] The famous Catholic biblicist, J. L. McKenzie, invites moral theologians to re-examine 'the question without prejudices and with attention to the study of the cultures'; the fundamental question is 'whether a cultural change can be imposed as a condition for baptism or not.'[12] Studies on the biblical problem examined in full awareness of the respective contexts and reflections fostered by sociology of cultures, are more and more numerous and shed new light on the problem in Africa.[13] Christian authors, however, are far from approving the idea that Christians actually living in a monogamous culture can one day return to polygamy. It is important to stress this point so that nobody should draw wrong conclusions for our ancient cultures of Europe and America.

The opinion of those who think that at the time of Christ not only was polygamy still legitimate but leviratic marriage in particular was even obligatory seems to be established. We can assume at least that the community of James still considered it so.

In conclusion I want to express my own opinion. The sacramentality of Christian marriage and the equal dignity of man and woman certainly fight in favour of monogamy as the norm or at least as a normative ideal towards which the Church should direct all her members. However, it is not for this reason that this norm should be imposed at once in every case and culture. Already in the Old Testament, marriage appeared as a sign of the alliance between God and his people and yet holy people, patriarchs and prophets, did not draw the conclusion from this that polygamy is totally against the gratuitous alliance of God. The obligation of conjugal fidelity was of great importance. All that Christ said against divorce should at least make us reflect with much care on the case of the peaceful and socially approved polygamous family found as such by the gospel; in this regard, I do not think one should, in the name of the Lord, impose divorce of the second wife as a condition for baptism.

Nevertheless, the reflection should not be made in abstract terms. Rather we should consider the strong tensions existing today in the African soul and the cultures which are still polygamous. In fact on one hand the tradition needs to be revalued, but at the same time on the other hand the instance of modern culture which tends especially to the recognition of the equal or practically equal role of the woman in society deserves to be accepted. And surely the admittance of the woman to cultural and professional formation gives a new motive for monogamy.

Today the Church has to fight against new forms of polygamy which are socially disapproved of and unacceptable. It should be remembered that in the Africa of old, polygamy was not sought for sexual satisfaction. The idea of pan-sexualism is altogether foreign to the greater part of African cultures. The intention was usually rather to guarantee for oneself the greatest number of children and to multiply friendships and alliances between clans. On the other hand, for some time there has been noticed, in the new urban centres, a tendency to imitate the licentiousness and to follow the sexual ideologies imported from North America and Europe. The Church has to fight a difficult battle. There is need of a high degree of discernment and education to discernment so as to find satisfying solutions for all.

On the presupposition that the universal Church recognizes a greater autonomy and pluralism of the local ecclesial communities, every diocese and each Bishops' Conference must consider the repercussions that their solution could have in neighbouring zones. A better knowledge of the interdependence

145

between the concrete culture and the norms which aim at the greatest possible good is therefore indispensable in the entire Church. So if, in a stage of primary evangelization, the Church permits a gradual pastoral practice even on a collective level, this cannot justify any community or person's permissive conduct on the grounds of the gradual pastoral and moral pedagogy which is valid for another zone. The dynamism of moral education allows patience, but not a regression.

Any question which is like the one of polygamy should be resolved within the framework of the mission confided to the Church: to make all nations disciples of Christ. Any suspicion or even the least shade of a colonialist attitude has to be excluded. The juridical norms and the concrete forms of moral and pastoral pedagogy existing on the European continent cannot automatically be exported to and imported by cultures which are quite different. The least that can be demanded is that the local Churches be allowed to reflect on such problems in sincerity and loyalty in order to suggest to the higher authorities solutions which, according to them, meet the demands of the gospel and the progressive growth of the Christian community and the society in general. The decisions should, however, not be imposed by one who has no profound knowledge of the various cultural situations for which they are promulgated.

B. *Sterile marriages*

In Africa, as in practically all the ancient cultures, the first purpose of marriage is procreation. This is true both for the polygamous marriage and for the monogamous one. The consequences which result from this, as we have already seen, are many: for example, the choice of a second wife who guarantees the traditional family the so much longed-for fecundity. In many regions a sterile marriage is automatically dissolved. This difference among the various tribes makes a very rigorous insistence on monogamy, leading practically to a cultural choice in the sense of the dissolution of marriages without offspring.

Thus face to face with the problem of fertility, we find ourselves before successive polygamy. In this context, the Christian ideal is evident: to project all the other ends of marriage, especially that of union, that is, the indissoluble bond and conjugal love. In some cases the Church has succeeded in making the indissolubility of the sterile marriage acceptable by promoting the practice of adoption.

In many African cultures, however, fertility enjoys so much appreciation that it is not possible, within a short time, to make the ideal of an indissoluble monogamy concretely acceptable when fertility is lacking. Even in the case where the spouses have solemnly sworn not to have any reserve about the indissolubility, the condition of fertility remains present and inscribed in the collective conscience and in all the structures of life.[14] Only great heroes could become pioneers of a gradual change.

My conviction, which is shared by many local Churches that I have visited or with which I have entered into correspondence, is that the immediate solution is not to refuse sacramental honour to the second marriage contracted after the dissolution of the first one which was sterile, at least in the case when the dissolution does not depend on the free choice of the spouse who now lives in a fertile marriage. In fact, according to the anthropological conditions of those cultures, absolute indissolubility belongs only to a fertile marriage. It is quite clear that a tradition of this type cannot be accepted as a norm for the Church. There is, however, need for a patient pedagogy in order to transform mental and cultural structures. After all, we must be very careful not to oppose the high appreciation given to offspring by these cultures, especially in view of the sad situation in the old continents of Europe and North America, where many family communities no longer know how to appreciate the true value of this gift of God; a juridical and moral rigorism could have such bad consequences when it discriminates sharply against spouses who, according to their custom and the collective conscience, live happily in a second marriage after the failure of the first which was sterile.

C. *Customary marriage; the conflict between the uniformity of canon law and customs regarding the celebration of marriage*

In the first millennium the evangelizing work of the Church

was very much favoured by lack of a uniform marriage law and of an invalidating sanction attached to a determined canonical form. The Church brought her message of the presence of Christ, of fidelity and of reconciliation to the marriage of the newly converted Christians, which continued to be contracted according to the traditional forms. However, when the European Church was to begin her mission in other cultures, the Council of Trent decreed a canonical form with the invalidating sanction. This law, which for a long time was applied in great parts of Europe, was observed everywhere as an absolute in the African missions.

The rigorous legislation of the code of canon law on mixed marriages seemed to be one of the major obstacles to ecumenical conciliation. In this field the Church has made a great advance. Nevertheless, for large parts of the world, the rigidity with which the celebration in the canonical form is demanded, is one of the major causes of alienation from the Church and an impediment to effective evangelization. The gospel of fidelity and redeeming love cannot be leaven to millions of marriages declared invalid by the ecclesiastical laws. The problem is an extremely urgent one in the Caribbean Islands, and in the greater part of Latin America and Africa. The obstacles are of different kinds; as an example I again give first attention to the African situation.

The greater part of the African cultures have traditions and concepts different from Roman ones. Everything proceeds according to customs and social controls which function within the family, and the social, cultural and economic system. There are determinate stages that the marriage must pass through before it arrives at its final solidity.[15] Normally, the definitive winning-post is arrived at only when the fertility is guaranteed and the bride price paid. However, in many tribes the couple initiate their conjugal life in an anterior phase. According to European categories this is judged as: 1) premarital sexual relations and fornication; 2) concubinage; 3) *trial marriage*. All these nomenclatures are offensive in regard to the African traditions. It is not a question of European and North American pre-marital sexual relations where there is a complete lack of social control. One cannot speak of concubinage either because by definition concubinage lacks the will towards stability.

Much less can one speak of *trial marriage*, for, in the propositions of the western libertines, to this belongs the unique status of experimentation without any further obligation, while in the African marriage all, from the beginning, is serious and motivated towards the final consolidation which takes place if there do not arise obstacles which are truly grave and rigorously weighed by custom. Through marriage, Africa knows something which can be compared to the temporary vows of religious congregations. The canonical form imposed from the first step in marriage is seen as a violent imposition contrary to the collective conscience and the traditional wisdom. In fact, in the last years the resistance has grown and a great majority of young Christians do not renounce the customary stages and the usual celebrations. Those who ignore the steps prescribed by the traditions are not considered truly married. On the one hand the young cannot detach themselves from the customs and the concepts of the patriarchal or matriarchal family, since that would otherwise bring a danger of breaking with the families that have prepared the marriage; yet on the other hand the clergy is also often reluctant to sanction the marriage immediately if, within the society, it is not yet considered as definitive and irrevocable. Often, people are afraid to make so sacred a promise before the altar, because they fear the terrible consequences in case they cannot maintain it, even if it is through no fault of theirs.[16]

In many regions of Africa, the Caribbean Islands and Latin America only a relative minority begin their conjugal life according to the Roman canon law, and it is often precisely these marriages which turn out to be the less stable as many studies have shown. And since the divorced persons practically always remarry, the number of those who are excluded from the sacraments of the Church, because of our concept of marriage, keeps growing more and more. In many local Churches the clergy has decided to give the sacramental celebration only to those young couples that have completed the traditional stages. Meanwhile, however, and this may last for some years, these couples are gradually considered as living 'in a state of mortal sin', so that those who want to remain faithful to their social and family community are excluded from the Eucharist, the great sign of the Christian community.

One cannot deny that this practically mechanical application of our marriage concept and law has contributed to the diminution of the stability of marriage in numerous zones of Africa.[17] A better knowledge of the general situation permits an evaluation of the traditional system more positive than the one given by missionaries who through no fault of their own were completely unprepared from the ethnological and anthropological point of view. 'There is no reason to think that African traditional marriage would be less effective as a stimulus to the exercising of human virtue than the matrimonial system of any other continent whatsoever.'[18]

To arrive at a more just appreciation of the African custom and in consideration of the failure of a legalistic imposition by a foreign system, the problem has been re-thought in some local Churches and a provisory solution found in this sense: it is required that the pastors, parish-priest and catechist, be informed, and that before cohabitation as husband and wife, the young couple present themselves to declare that it is firmly decided to tend towards the finalization of the marriage as soon as possible, according to the customs and if no unsurmountable obstacle arises. Meanwhile this couple will be following the courses on conjugal and family life. This phase thus becomes a kind of catechumenate for marriage.

It should also be noted that this problem becomes more and more complicated because of the dynamic transformation of the African cultures. In various nations the young generation is in full rebellion against the system of dowry, which is often exaggerated and subjected to the rigid control of the families. Thus young people live together without observing the customary states and refuse the institution of the dowry. In some local Churches the clergy remain attached to the old traditions and so refuse ecclesiastical marriage to one who is not ready to observe these old traditions. This is another cause of the great number of canonically invalid marriages often unfortunately considered on the same footing as 'concubinage'. Thus the ecclesiastical sanctions often obtain results contrary to what they intended to obtain.

I do not possess magical formulas for solving all these problems. However it can be affirmed with certainty that the authority of the universal Church should concede to the local

Churches a greater liberty for solving these complex problems according to the real possibilities. This will also encourage a gradual pedagogy which corresponds to the whole context of the culture in question. In my humble opinion the Church would only have everything to gain if she would restore the situation that existed (on this particular question) before the Council of Trent. No marriage should be declared invalid when it concerns a form that is socially approved and controlled and has proper sacramental intentions. The Church should meet with sympathy customs in their dynamism and be present to every serious marriage with the pedagogy of faith and morals.[19]

The fundamental principle for the admission to the sacraments will always be that of the Christmas message: 'Peace on earth to men of good will'. In order to judge what is humanly possible or impossible the knowledge, not only of man in the abstract or of the European, but of everywhere people taken in their concrete historical context, is necessary. It is demanded of us as Europeans that we abandon the temptation to impose our mental, social and juridical structures on cultures for which they are not made and on men and women whom the Creator, Lord of history, has certainly not designed for such structures.

NOTES

1 Among the many studies on this question are: A. Hastings, *Christian Marriage in Africa*, London, 1973; W. G. Blum, *The unity of Christian marriage considered in relation to the polygamous cultures of Uganda*, Kisubu/Uganda, 1972; (extract of doctoral thesis discussed at the Accademia Alfonsiana); E. N. Kofon, *Polygyny in pre-Christian Bafut and the new moral theological perspective*, Doctoral dissertation, Accademia Alfonsiana, 1974; E. Hillman, *The Church as Mission*, New York, 1965, 'Polygyny Reconsidered', in *Practical Anthropology XVII*, 2 (March-April 1970). Also in *Concilium*, March 1968, 'Polygamy Reconsidered'.

2 B. Häring, 'Contestation missionaire de la morale chrétienne', in *Spiritus, Cahiers de Spiritualité missionaire* 10 (1969, pp. 38, 150–157) reprinted in 'Missionary Dimension of Protest', in: *A Theology of Protest*, New York, 1970, pp. 137–150, expresses the endurance and the perplexity of many missionaries.

3 Cf. A. Hastings, *Christian Marriage in Africa*, p. 7ff.

4 Cf. L. Newbigin, *La Chiesa missionaria nel mondo moderno*, p. 108ff: 'none of those who know the modern mission can deny that legalism constitutes one of the biggest problems, the tragic consequences of imposing on the new Christian communities a moral norm that they cannot accept spontaneously. . . Let us think, for example, of the tragic history of the fight against polygamy in Africa, where the mission wanted to make monogamy a law, before the newly converted knew all the consequences.'

5 Cf. A. Hastings, *op. cit.*, p. 20ff.
6 W. G. Blum, *op. cit.*, opts for this solution, accepting theoretically the practice of the diocese in which he exercises his ministry. The African is not attracted by this solution because he resents the abnormal situation of being a catechumen all his life.
7 This point is clearly treated by E. N. Kogfon, *op. cit.*
8 A. Hastings, *op. cit.*, p. 77.
9 'There should, nevertheless, be very real sympathy for Christians who at present, in conformity with the past custom of their people, decide with the willing agreement of the first wife to take a second in the circumstances of childlessness, the widowhood of a sister-in-law, and, perhaps, the acceptance of an obviously handicapped girl' (A. Hastings, *op. cit.*, p. 78). He came to this conclusion after having patiently explored the reflections of the Catholic and Anglican Churches of East and South Africa.
10 E. Schillebeeckx, *Marriage: Secular Reality and Saving Mystery*, London, 1965. I, 284.
11 Cf. J. Jeremias, *Jerusalem in the Time of Jesus*, London, 1965, pp. 93-94.
12 Cf. J. L. McKenzie in *The Critic*, Nov.-Dec. 1970, p. 95.
13 Cf. H. Ringeling, 'Die biblische Begründung der Monogamie', in *Zeitschrift für Evangelische Ethik* 10 (1966), pp. 81-102; R. Hoslst, 'Polygamy and the Bible', in *International Review of Missions* 56 (1967), pp. 205-213; L. Newbigin, *Honest Religion for Secular Man*, London, 1966, pp. 72-74; M. Buthelizi, 'Polygyny in the Light of the New Testament', in *African Theological Journal* 1 (1969), pp. 58-70.
14 Cf. M. Hauben, *Contribution à la solution de la problématique du mariage africain et de son paiement*, Rome, 1966, extract from laureal dissertation presented at the Accademia Alfonsiana, 1964.
15 Cf. A. Philips (editor), *Survey of African Marriage and Family Life*, London, 1953; A. Hastings, *op. cit.*, pp. 21ff; T. Olawale Ellas, *The Nature of African Customary Law*, Manchester, 1954; J. Zoa, 'La Dot dans les territoires d'Afrique', in *Femmes Africaines*, Paris, 1959, pp. 53-71.
16 Cf. A. Hastings, *op. cit.*, p. 50.
17 *Ibid.*, p. 50.
18 *Ibid.*, p. 37.
19 *Ibid.*, p. 72.

5

The ministry of peace and reconciliation in a lacerated world

The three most urgent concerns which characterize this last decade of our millennium are: 1) healing liberation from violence in all its forms, especially from the worst of its historical Hydras: the mutually assured threat of destruction by nuclear and other mass destructive weapons, which could destroy all life on this planet; 2) the scandalous imbalance between the extremely poor and the starving nations of the South and the industrially highly developed countries which get deadly sick because of ruthless competition, unhealthy life-styles and lack of wisdom; 3) the idol of ever growing production and consumption, rooted in a success-oriented system of education which threatens the basic conditions of life on earth.

This decade towards the third Christian millennium may decide whether humanity will grow in wisdom and responsibility as stewards of the created world entrusted to us by our Creator or commit the greatest blasphemy against the Creator by devastating and finally destroying the very conditions of life on earth. Will Christians, united in conversion and reconciliation, be able to witness to the gospel of peace and its path: active nonviolence? Will we be able, with the weapons of peace and nonviolence, to fight individual and collective egotism in favour of saving solidarity? Will we firmly decide to make wise use of the gifts of the Creator by sharing and by a healthy, simple life-style? Will we prepare a nonviolent world culture for the third Christian millennium? This is a matter of 'to be or not to be'.

1. *The general picture*

In the analysis made by the chapter introducing the pastoral constitution *Gaudium et spes*, the term 'imbalance' recurs often. A world which is involved in a rapid and profound transformation feels more the imbalance which is ultimately caused, even if not uniquely, by sin.

Every sin is at the same time a cause and an expression of division, tension, breaking apart. Man is divided even in the most intimate depths of his own existence. The apostle of the Gentiles describes life, even that of the redeemed, as a fight between spirit and incarnate egoism (*sarx*). The battle between these two modes of existence involves people in such a remarkable way because the forces of the Spirit and incarnate egoism find themselves face to face in the world.

The more man follows the direction of incarnate egoism, bearing the bitter fruits of it, the more these lacerations become manifest. 'Anyone can see the behaviour that belongs to the selfish nature . . . quarrels, a contentious temper, envy, fits of rage, selfish ambitions, dissensions, party intrigues and jealousies' (Gal 5: 19–20). The same Paul had much to suffer seeing how the seeds of discord grew even in the Churches founded by him.

Sin instals itself as loveless dispute, division or disruption in families, social classes, nations, in relations between different states and cultures and, unfortunately frequently today, even within the Church, local and universal, where there are sharp tensions between various currents. Sin has expressed itself as a profound tearing of the mystical Body of Christ especially in the schisms and strifes, sometimes very intense, between the different parts of Christianity.

At the present moment we are witnessing one of the most dangerous explosions of contention and hatred between adherents of two monotheistic religions, Jews and Muslims; and both parties claim the honour of having Abraham as father. . . While they express their faith in only one God, they sacralize their hatred and antagonism. And in fact, in the diversity of their temperaments and capacities, they could be for each other a gift of God. Thanks be to God that many Jews and Muslims are beginning to realize this.

National and international conflicts become particularly treacherous because of an unusual mixing of the interests of groups, ideologies, and beliefs. The most clear example is the

154

one from the middle-east, but also relevant in this regard are the fights in Northern Ireland, South Africa, Lebanon, Afghanistan and the opposition between the communist world and the western world. Co-existence is so difficult because the egotistic interests are skillfully hidden behind ideologies. And besides the perverse ideologies are also found, on one side or the other, some authentic ideals and some preoccupation for absolutely incontestable values.

The world is divided between rich and poor, privileged and discriminated against, organized and powerful social classes and others neither organized nor truly represented. Not only do we find ourselves before grave tensions between young and old, but we also witness crazy hostilities against those who are the weakest and most innocent, children not yet born. And these conflicts interlace with those between the old castes and tribes and the new cultures, between a world economically developed, but poor regarding wisdom, and people deprived of the means of livelihood.

An important part of humanity has been liberated from that intolerance which was the cause of so much fanaticism, and led to the Inquisition, torture and religious wars. However, that does not take away the fact that we still stand before new forms of intolerance, based either on legalism or on that vague liberalism which is a complete ideological relativism and does not support the community of believers who firmly commit themselves to their faith, looking for opportunities to witness to it and to communicate it to others. Ideological relativism transforms itself into dogma, most intolerant towards believers, because it excludes the existential search for the truth which saves and unites.

The summit of the situation of conflict consits in the tendency of one part of mankind to sacralize powers and violent conflict as new idols.

Different forms of Marxism and neo-Marxism see in the aggravation of the fight between social classes and ideologies and also in growing hatred, the internal law of history which guarantees by itself the true progress and hope of the future. It is in this way that there was presented to the world a new and peculiar 'doctrine of salvation' which, not only theoretically but also with the use of the most powerful means of

155

communication and with the organization of all the politico-economical forces, searches to impose belief in the conflict as the principal hope of humanity. The strange situation of today is then indicated by a post-revolutionary bureaucracy, which amalgamates with different forms of nationalism, and which, with the help of intellectuals, tries to spread this doctrine of salvation through progressive hatred and contention, among new generations and countries which still enjoy a certain liberty, while on the other hand it crushes every expression of opposition to such a doctrine and to its power, where it is in power. The roughest forms of authoritarianism wage a ruthless war against those socialist movements which search for gradual reforms and prefer nonviolent means. On this point we see now new signs of hope.

The sin of the world profits by numerous occasions to organize individuals and groups against each other. The confusion in the big cities with an inhuman density of population makes many people vulnerable to the temptation of violence or downright terrorism. Criminal gangs are organized by utopian fanatics who think they must increase the spiral of violence in order to prepare a new world. The number of psychopaths, who allow themselves to be manipulated in this way, keeps growing. Then some simple-minded people easily insert themselves into this tendency, using jargon which prefers words such as 'rupture' or 'conflict' without explaining their content and intentionality.

The complexity of all these phenomena of laceration, division and rupture does not permit an easy and optimistic way. In fact, we should only be very pessimistic if we did not have the gospel of reconciliation, which is not just a remote and quasi-foreign word to us, but is in fact an incarnate reality in our world and in human history.

2. *The response: the gospel of reconciliation*

Where the conflict abounds, there superabounds grace which can lead us to peace and reconciliation. The forces of conflict are powerless before Christ who is the peace and reconciliation offered by the Father and who is always at work in the world. This period of battle and tension is a great test of our faith. It can be a challenge and a *kairos* which solicits from us a more grateful and involved acceptance of the gift of reconciliation.

A. *The meaning of 'reconciliation' in scripture*

In the religion of Israel, as in any other religion, the idea of reconciliation with God is one of the primary preoccupations: people seek for God's favour through suitable rites and good works. The *characteristics* of the revealed religion, however, which through the prophets became ever clearer till it obtained its fulfilment in Jesus Christ, is that the subject of reconciliation is not man but God himself. It is God who reveals himself as favourable, and invites people to reconciliation with him and with others. 'Human activity, including penance and the confession of sins, is not primarily something in which man takes the initiative in order to be reconciled with God, a human work to which God would respond; it is rather already a reaction, or a human response, which becomes possible and obligatory because God offers the gift of reconciliation.'[1]

It should be noted that the New Testament rarely uses the words *hilaskomai, hilasmos, hilasterion,*[2] which in Greek culture indicate the reconciliating rites in which man is conceived as the subject while God is considered as the object (*hilaskomai*, to propitiate, conciliate; *hilasmos*, expiation, propitiation; and *hilasterion*, that which expiates or propitiates). In the passages in which these terms are used, the context underlines clearly the divine initiative. '. . . They are justified by his grace as a gift, through the redemption which is in Christ Jesus, whom God put forward as an expiation (*hilasterion*) by his blood, to be received by faith. This was to show God's righteousness, because in his divine forbearance he has passed over former sins; it was to prove at the present time that he himself is righteous and that he justifies him who has faith in Jesus (cf. Rom 3 : 24–26).

In non-biblical Greek the word *apocatastasis,*[3] reconstitution or reconciliation, has often a political or an apocalyptical sense. Even in this sense biblical use of it is sparing, because the New Testament tends to exclude every false idea of messianism, in the sense of a political or nationalist messiah. The verb *apocatistanai*, to restore or reconcile all, is also little used. In the Acts of the Apostles it appears once and expresses that expectation of the disciples which is re-oriented by Jesus: they asked Christ before his ascension, 'Lord, is this the time when you are to establish once again the sovereignty of Israel?' (Acts 1 : 6). The response draws attention to the work of the Holy Spirit who transforms the apostles into witnesses. Even in Mt 17 : 11, the Lord corrected the wrong idea of those who were expecting Elijah to come back to restore the power of Israel. The term *apocatastasis* is used only in Acts 3 : 21, where it speaks of the return of Christ who died and rose to accomplish his work of redemption and reconciliation. The content of the hope of *apocatastasis* in the classical sense (final restitution or reconciliation) is however presented in the first letter to the Corinthians. 'When all things are subjected to him, then the Son himself will also be subjected to him who put all things under him, that God may be everything to every one' (1 Cor 15 : 28). Even here the emphasis is on the divine initiative and every idea of a political messianism is eliminated.

The terms that Paul prefers are *katalloghè, katallassein*[4] and so on. They were until then used only in profane life, never for propitiary rites. In Greek, the words express the reconciliation of men in daily life: between families and between peoples. The fact that the apostle used terms which do not make one think in the first place of a rite stresses the universal character connected with them. Each time Paul uses the word 'reconciliation', he emphasizes the divine initiative and the gratuitous gift in relation with faith which is the humble and grateful acceptance of the good news of salvation and reconciliation, and answer through one's entire life. Reconciliation does not have only a vertical direction, but is an all-embracing reality. The classical text is found in 2 Corinthians 5 : 13–21: the blood of the alliance, the propitiatory death, is the true reconciliation and the overcoming of all egoism which divides the hearts of persons and societies. 'For the love of Christ controls us, because we are convinced that one has died for all; therefore all have died. And he died for all, that those who live might live no longer for themselves but for him who for their sake died and was raised. From now on, therefore, we regard no one from a human point of view; even though we once regarded Christ from a human point of view; we regard him thus no longer. Therefore if anyone is in Christ, he is a new creation; the old has passed away, behold, the new has come. All this is from God, who through Christ reconciled us to himself and gave us the ministry of reconciliation; that is, God was in Christ reconciling the world to himself, not counting their trespasses against them, and entrusting to us the message of reconciliation' (2 Cor 5 : 14–19). 'The horizon of reconciliation is indeed as vast as the amplitude of the whole of creation.'[5]

The whole world should profit by the peace and reconciliation which is offered to us in Jesus Christ. Reconciliation with God is, however, not possible without accepting the gracious call to reconciliation between people and commitment to the world created by God for the benefit of all and entrusted to humankind to be administered in wisdom and by generous sharing of God's gifts. It is the very gift of God which motivates and obliges Christians to reconcile themselves and to remove the cause of all division and contention. Paul considered himself as an ambassador of Christ the reconciler, and implored all in the name of the Lord saying: 'So we are ambassadors for Christ, God making his appeal through us' (2 Cor 5 : 20).

Paul VI, who draws from the gift the pleasant obligation of gratitude and acceptance, expresses himself in this sense, faithful to the mind of the apostle. 'We need to re-establish authentic, vital and happy relations with God, to be reconciled with him, in humility and love, so that from this first constitutional harmony, our whole world of experience may express one demand and acquire one virtue — reconciliation, in charity and justice, with men whom we immediately recognize under the new title of brothers. Reconciliation occurs on other very wide and real levels, on the levels of the ecclesial community itself, of society, of politics, of ecumenism and of peace.'[6]

All the quarrels and dissensions and all the ideologies which glorify strife and violence cannot make us pessimistic, because there is before us reconciliation and peace in Jesus Christ who took upon himself the situation of conflict even to the shedding of his blood, the blood of the new and everlasting covenant. The acceptance of reconciliation is a total conversion to Christ and unites us with his paschal mysteries, prepares us to suffer with Christ, to conquer hatred, to bless those who persecute us and to love our enemies, in order to establish on earth the justice which Jesus brought.

The biblical message of reconciliation is such that it does not allow any evasion. The totality of the gift demands a full gratitude and undivided engagement in one's own conversion and in the renewal of the whole of life with a clear scope of reconciling all people to God and to each other.

B. *The Church, the sacrament of reconciliation*

The Church is the called, the convoked one of Christ, who invites Jews and Gentiles, Greeks and non-Greeks, slaves and freedmen to unity. She is the place in which reconciliation with God is manifested because, in the faith in one Father and in one Lord and Reconciler, Jesus Christ, and through the grace of the Holy Spirit, believers unite together in a community of salvation; while, according to the fruit of incarnate egoism (*sarx*), they would have strong motives of separation and reciprocal discrimination. The presence of Christ is for his disciples a continuous call to reconciliation. Thus the Chruch is capable of carrying out her great mission, not only to announce but also to work for the reconciliation given us in the Word (cf. 2 Cor 5 : 18), if she renews herself in humble and grateful acceptance of the gift of peace.

In the intention and with the abundant grace of God, the Church is an efficacious and visible sign of the reconciliation offered to the whole world. But because of the sins of her members and, sometimes, of her leaders, sins which are associated with the lacerating solidarity of the sin of the world, she is not always and everywhere a truly efficacious and visible sacrament of reconciliation. The great obstacles to reconciliation and peace are always sins, and sins especially of Christians. Above all, dissensions, destructive criticism and divisions between groups are grave contradictions of the mission of the Church to be the sacrament of reconciliation for the whole world. One of the most urgent demands of the Christian faith is therefore to endeavour continuously and with self-denial to create harmony within Christianity.

The schisms and separations within Christianity are sins of ingratitude towards God and infidelity to our mission to be signs of the reconciled people of God. Ecumenism, the effort towards reconciliation and towards the reunion of the various parts, thus becomes an urgent appeal of the gift of reconciliation and the mission itself of the Church, and also a duty of gratitude towards God and responsibility towards the world.[7] Ecumenism should always proceed at equal pace with patient effort which aims at attuning the different tendencies in the Church and overcoming the polarizations which do not express an acceptable pluralism but are rather fruit of egoism and partial blindness.

C. *The sacramentalization of the ministry of reconciliation*

Before speaking of the sacraments or of a sacrament of reconciliation, we are obliged to speak of the Church which is meant to be and to become evermore, in all her life, mission and sacrament of reconciliation. However, as this concerns the Church who adores God in spirit and truth, and renders visible the gratuity of the gift through the sacraments, her mission expresses itself particularly, if not exclusively, in the sacraments oriented towards life. An attitude which, in regard to the sacraments, makes one forget the duty of the reconciliation of the world and all mankind to God and in their own relations is not valid. And since the Church is integrally called to be sacrament of reconciliation, all her sacraments proclaim and signify the same message in and through the different sectors and situations of life.

Baptism unites Christians to that of Christ, which is not only a baptism in water, but in water, in blood and in the Spirit for the reconciliation of all (cf. 1 Jn 5:6). Insertion in the baptism of Christ is grace and mission to become part of the Church, sacrament of unity in the midst of the conflicts of the world.

The Eucharist is above all the celebration of the great event of reconciliation and therefore a thanksgiving which necessarily becomes a proclamation, and an active ministry for the sake of the ecclesial community and of the whole of humanity.

Marriage is the image of the covenant between Christ and the Church, an alliance which endures because the Lord reconciles, pardons and always re-inserts his Church in his own reconciling work. Thus to enter into marriage becomes a duty always to forgive generously and to be ever ready for reconciliation. If the announcement and ministry of reconciliation were the golden rule and *leitmotif* of all Christian life, many marriages would be more stable because there would be created a continuous influence towards being faithful to the marriage alliance in forgiving love.

I have often tried to explain the sacrament of penance as, 'the sacrament of reconciliation and of peace'.[8] In fact, it does not concern penance in the first place, but the grace of Christ which reconciles us with God the Father and with the ecclesial community in view of our mission of witnessing and promoting reconciliation and peace. In the celebration of the sacrament of reconciliation, the central point should therefore be the great commandment of love whose value is tested in the conditions of conflict which demand pardon and help so as to be overcome. In this perspective a higher appreciation both of fraternal correction and of revision of life or the community celebration of this sacrament should certainly be encouraged. This would make every dimension of the celebration of the mystery better understood. This is one of the main orientations in the new liturgical legislation about the sacrament of reconciliation.

The sacrament of holy orders is bound in a particular manner to the mission of the Church: that is, to be the announcing and carrying out of reconciliation. For such a ministry the choice should therefore fall on those who have, in a particular way, the charism of reconciling their brethren. Above all, at this historical moment which is so charged with tensions, the priest will have to pay great attention to his role as reconciler and educator of his brethren in reconciliation. He should not think only of the rare and exceptional cases, but also of the small disturbances or difficulties of daily life.

D. *A decisive decade of reconciliation*

We read the gospel of peace and reconciliation in fullest awareness that this last decade of our millennium is the greatest challenge to Christians and all believers in God, the Creator and Redeemer. We are to be converted to truthful faith in the One God and Creator by grateful and responsible sharing of his gifts, by striving towards a culture characterized by learning how to be wise and imploring this high gift from God. We are to be thoroughly converted to God's plan of salvation announced in the four songs of the Servant of God and witnessed by Christ unto death on the cross: the road of saving, healing, liberating nonviolence that calls even enemies to friendship.

It is in this *kairos*, in this challenging and favourable moment, that we understand the urgency of the gospel appeal: 'You are the light of the world, the salt of the earth'.

Praising God's wisdom and mercy we have to confess our sins, not only our individual sins, but our manifold ways of involvement in collective egotism, injustice, violence, exploitation, clinging even to sinful structures in Church and society.

The Churches, universal and local, should examine their whole life deeply to see if they really express the *kerygma* and the ministry of reconciliation in the world in such a way as to respond to the signs of the times. It is an opportune moment for reflection on how the Church with her diverse parts, currents, cultures and subcultures conducts herself in the difficult search for new ways to express the same message in the diversity of languages and new cultures. It cannot be a question of a return to that unity which was conceived too statically and according to a uniform scheme. We must live the plurality of expressions in the unity of faith. This is possible only if we always look for unity in charity, in mutual respect and understanding. It means above all an examination of conscience on how we resolve situations of conflict. Often we must stir up the tranquil unity of a group, of a social class or even of a clergy which acts in such a manner that it withdraws itself from the masses, from the working class and from the poor. We must ask ourselves how we can bring apprehension where there is unjustified calm, and work so as really to contribute towards a larger and more complete reconciliation of the whole of humanity.

How do we react in social conflicts? We certainly cannot invite the exploited, the oppressed and those at the fringe of society to be happy with their situation. On the contrary we must loyally associate ourselves with them in their demands for greater justice and in their fight for equal rights. We must, however, humanize these struggles, that is, we must permeate them with the leaven of interior peace, healing benevolence, justice towards all and the will to fight with arms of justice and of active nonviolence. Our times are ones of nonviolent revolutions. We can unmask the ideologies which put their confidence in violent and cruel upheavals only if we succeed in showing the forcefulness of the great revolution of the gospel, in justice and in reconciliation. The desire to manifest our gratitude to God who has reconciled us to himself must always and everywhere be present through our generous and patient engagement in reconciliation with others, while we are at the same time mediators and channels of peace in situations of conflict. This should be a characteristic of our spirituality at this historical moment.[9]

E. *Education towards reconciliation*

1. *Education towards dialogue* — The universal ministry of reconciliation demands a special effort to educate ourselves in the virtue and art of dialogue. The first encyclical of Paul VI, *Ecclesiam suam*, makes a great contribution to the vision of dialogue in view of reconciliation. Dialogue is, in the first place, the capacity to listen to others with the desire to understand them. Therefore, attention is not paid only to the words, but also to the entire situation of the life of a person, in his or her sufferings and whole experience. Dialogue is a virtue only when it does not remain just on the level of abstract ideas, but is willing and determined to respond to other people generously and with commitment.

Dialogue is the art of sharing experiences and reflections in order to reach a more complete vision of the world which leads to a more lucid commitment to a better world. Dialogue should also always be the purpose of any contestation. Any form of criticism or protest which makes a fruitful dialogue more difficult or completely impossible is not a virtue, but a vice.[10]

A fruitful dialogue is possible only when there is a will to come together for the purpose of the gradual realization of our ideals and the rights of all.

Dialogue is the expression of the reciprocity of consciences which are united in the search for truth and valid solutions to the problems which continually arise in individual and social life (cf. *Gaudium et spes*, 16).

2. *Reconciling tolerance* — The virtue of tolerance has its vital place in a humble search for truth and for just solutions to the great problems of life. True tolerance has nothing in common with the indifferentism which is not concerned with truth or does not believe in truth or in values to which we must submit ourselves to be truly human. Fanatical intolerance which has characterized long periods of the history of religions and their antagonisms has been the result of an arbitrary identification of conceptualizations with truth itself. Intolerance is the result of individual and collective price. Modern indifferentism which becomes arrogance, contempt and intolerance towards the faithful manifests self-pride. The relativists and those indifferent in regard to truth often claim for themselves the right of infallibility when they assert that truth cannot be known. To overcome the old intolerance and to avoid the new intolerant indifferentism, the faithful need a high degree of mutual respect and discernment.[11]

3. *A nonviolent active engagement* — The Christian shall not allow illusions of any kind in regard to reconciliation. It is a work of Christ which cost him the shedding of his blood. Thus the Lord has become the revelation of peace, reconciliation and the victory of love in the great conflict between the new creation and incarnate egoism. His reconciling work does not permit passivity or evasion, but implies the most active presence of nonviolent action for justice which unmasks all the injustices present in a sinful world. We cannot demythologize the most insidious Marxist ideology if we do not oppose it with something other than a mean preoccupation with our own security, which is prone to the accepting of an unjust order or a pessimistic evasion. Only those Christians who witness to justice in firm solidary action can

overthrow the modern idols of violence and overcome systematic hatred.[12]

A theoretical choice of the poor is not sufficient; the conversion of the rich, the powerful and the privileged is necessary. The fight of the oppressed alone for liberation and for the obtaining of their own rights is not in itself a sign of the kingdom of God. But if the rich, the powerful and the privileged are converted to justice and to the evangelical beatitudes, committing themselves to the good of the poor, the oppressed and those discriminated against, then we have a sure testimony to the coming of God's kingdom.

For example, in the racist or colonized countries of Africa it should not be the Africans who should carry the greatest burden of the struggle for justice: it should be the whites and those who exercise power that should leave their arms aside and generously meet their brethren. This would be reconciliation according to the gift offered us by the Father in Christ. Utopia? We need first of all courageous and enthusiastic vanguards.

We do not carry in ourselves the gift and power of reconciliation. To be able to be ministers and ambassadors of it we must live in the word of Christ. A reconciling presence in the conflicts of the world is not possible if we do not live a life of faith and prayer, a life of contemplation which acts and loves without allowing evasions, because we are inserted in the mission of the incarnate Word.

NOTES

1 H. Vorländer, 'Versöhnung', in *Theologisches Begriffslexikon zum Neuen Testament* (edited by L. Coenen, E. Beyreuther and H. Bietenhard), Wuppertal, 1971, II/2, p. 1308.

2 For *hilaskomai* cf. H. G. Link, 'Vorsöhnung', in *op. cit.*, pp. 1304-1307.

3 Cf. A. Oepke, 'Apokathistemi', etc., in *Theologisches Wörterbuch zum NT*, I, 1933, pp. 386-392; H. Vorländer — H. G. Link, 'Versöhung, in *Theol. Begriffslexikon zum* NT, II/2, pp. 1302-1313.

4 Cf. F. Büchsel, '*Alasso*', in *Theologisches Wörterbuch zum NT*, I, 1933, pp. 252-260; K. Barth, *Die Lehre von der Versöhnung. Kirchliche Dogmatik*, 1953-1959, Vol. IV/1, IV/2, IV/3; V. Taylor, *Forgiveness and Reconciliation*, London, 1946; G. W. H. Lampe, *Reconciliation in Christ*, London, 1956; J. Dupont, *La Reconciliation dans la théologie de St-Paul*, Paris, 1953.

5 J. Moltmann, 'Gott versöhnt und macht frei', in *Evangelische Kommentare* 3 (1970), p. 517.

6 Paul VI, in *L'Osservatore Romano*, May 10, 1973.

7 Cf. B. Häring, *Prospettive e problemi ecumenici di teologia morale*, Rome, 1973.
8 Cf. B. Häring, *Shalom: Peace — the Sacrament of Reconciliation*, Garden City, New York, 1969; *Sin in the Secular Age*, St Paul Publications, Slough, 1974, pp. 212-214.
9 Cf. B. Haring, *The Healing Power of Peace and Nonviolence*, St Paul Publications, Slough, 1986.
10 Cf. A. Grabner-Haider, 'Kritik in der Kirche. Chancen und Misslingen eines Sprechaktes', in *Theologie der Gegenwart* 16 (1974), pp. 227-232.
11 Cf. chapter 1 of part III.
12 Cf. J. Thekkinedath, *Love of Neighbour in Mahatma Gandhi*, Alwaye/Kerala, 1973, dissertation, Accademia Alfonsiana.

CONCLUSION

A hope-filled vision of the Church
of the twenty-first century

A hope-filled vision

Dear reader, don't think that after all my life-experience I am
an optimist. I do dare to look into the face of shocking things,
such as a frosty near future in the Church:

We are approaching the peak of a century-long collective
'paternalistic neurosis' which somehow afflicts all of us, but
especially numerous members of the middle and higher clergy:
people who still 'believe' in triumphalistic, antibiblical honours
and titles; in male-power in the Church; who are anguished
by the mere thought of seeing a girl as an 'altar-girl'; are scan-
dalized by any kind of feminist theology as much as by liberation theology; they detest any pluralism in Church philosophy
and theology as much as in Church structures which they see as
a threat to their paternalistic security complex.

Be sure I am not blind about this and about a still widespread 'power-thinking' — a remnant of the centuries in which
popes, bishops and even monasteries were privileged and com-
peting allies of earthly monarchies, structured into the image
of 'this-worldly powers'.

My reasons for a hope-filled vision are stronger and of
another kind: I do believe in the gospel of Jesus Christ; I trust
in his promises and in the liberating and healing grace of his
Spirit. My hope-filled vision was strengthened by the experience
of the Second Vatican Council, by my many ecumenical experiences, by my friendship with wonderful bishops, priests
and religious, by looking at the many new forms of vocation
among the laity of all Churches. But the courage to suggest
the following hope-filled vision of the Church for the twenty-
first century, is above all, a kind of profession of my faith
and my trust in divine promises.

169

A Eucharistic Church

Since I believe strongly in the great Testament of Jesus Christ who left us the Eucharist as the greatest sign of his abiding love and faithfulness and as a gift for all believers, 'Take and eat of it: all of you', I dare to hope and must hope that early in the twenty-first century, in spite of the present reluctance of many, all Christian communities, above all those in the Catholic Church will have their Eucharistic ministers, so that all believers have everywhere and at all times the opportunity to share in the Eucharistic memorial.

No longer will man-made traditions, precious as they might have been in past centuries, block the solemn mandate and Testament 'eat and drink . . . *all of you*'.

Believers everywhere, experiencing that Church authorities in faithfulness to the Lord's mandate and covenant will overcome their own laziness and superficiality regarding participation in the Eucharist and tear down the artificial barriers which in the present frosty decade still make regular sharing in the Eucharist impossible.

There will be also a much better and much more profound appreciation of celibacy for the sake of God's Kingdom, celibacy freely chosen trusting in the grace of the Spirit, celibacy not imposed as a law and absolute condition for the Eucharistic ministry, but implored as a charism, accepted gratefully as undeserved charism, setting people free for a strong love for the unloved, for the poor, for the down-trodden, for those despised by the self-righteous.

The Eucharist accessible to all, understood by all as the Lord's solemn Testament and grace-filled mandate will be determining for the vision of spirituality and moral theology. The main criteria and motives of Christian life will be a 'grateful memory', the spirit of sharing in gratitude, sharing of the earthly goods as well of the charisms.

Mystery of faith

The emphasis by the shepherds of the Church, or better the good shepherds *within* the Church, will not be on obedience to the magisterium, but on 'knowing' the Master, whose 'mystery of faith' we celebrate. No man-made tradition will hide the depth and attractive beauty of faith. We believe above all in the 'mystery of faith' which in its depth and centre is *ineffable*. The whole Church, all Churches faithful to the Lord's Testament and mandate, 'That all may be one!', will be most careful not to impose a 'whole system' of time-bound concepts and definitions fabricated in a past European model of thought. Prime importance will be given to our shared adoration of the 'mystery of faith', the adoration of the Triune God, who is ever infinitely greater than all man-made concepts and definitions. Lived faith-experience, witness and symbols will play a greater role than precise 'concepts'.

Joyous celebration and joyous proclamation of good news

The Church, understanding herself above all as a Eucharistic community and shaped in her innermost being by the celebration and proclamation of the mystery of faith, will no longer feel the need to impose hundreds of moral norms as controllable burdens in matters in which she has no divine assurance and no convincing arguments. People formed in their heart and mind by a 'Eucharistic' grateful memory and by awe in the adoration of the mystery of faith, by a Spirit of praise and joy will live a much better and far more joyous Christian life, will be more convinced and convincing witnesses of the gospel than people being constantly plagued by paternalistic, patriarchal 'collective neurosis'. Moral pedagogy, moral preaching and scientific moral theology will be deeply marked by the gospel and by the joy and strength of faith in the liberating power and grace of the Holy Spirit.

There will be much more emphasis on and care to strengthen the spirit of joy, praise and adoration, and the faith in the ever greater mystery than an anxious and anguish-nourishing system of correct formulations in a uniformly applied fashion. The Spirit of Pentecost will reign speaking in all languages to people of all cultures. The Spirit will speak through the Eucharistic communities and Eucharistic people empowering all human endowment: memory (fantasy), imagination and

171

affection will lead to a better use of intelligence and will; purity of heart will receive greater attention.

The radiance of the basic communities and the local Churches

As soon as the Church, overcoming paternalistic neurosis, has provided enough good Eucharistic ministers for all communities and manifests the faithful exercise of subsidiarity and collegiality she will be fully open to the promptings of the Holy Spirit. Lust for power, for control and titles of honour will be unmasked as neurosis and anti-evangelical. Then an atmosphere of mutual trust will flourish at all levels between the successor of St Peter and the most humble people in the 'lowest' ranks. It will be an age of humility and simplicity. The small communities as well as the large ones will have their pastors whom they trust and whom they want.

The successor of Peter will gladly renounce the rather modern privilege of nominating all the bishops around the world. Why should Chinese bishops be 'created' in Rome and by Rome? Why should the bishop of Rome (called by the Master to preside over the ecumenical endeavour) be elected only by men 'created' and nominated by the past Pope?'New wine in new skins'. Let the Spirit work in all, through all, for the benefit of all. As soon as we have unmasked the anguishing game of paternalistic neurosis and the special historical causes of the collective neurosis in the 'Palace of the Roman Inquisition', the universal Church and the local Churches in all their relationships will become models testifying to the coming of God's liberating and healing reign.

As soon as the local Churches and the basic communities are experienced as Eucharistic communities of faith, hope and love, the Church at every level, in its breadth and depth, will get rid of any kind of inherited triumphalism and self-righteousness; we all shall be able to face the shades and errors of the past. Even on the institutional levels the confusion of faults, past and present, will free us for new dimensions of repentance, conversion, renewal and rethinking. The divisive walls between the different Churches, different cultures and, last but not least, between male and female, will fall. A better intelligence will prevail about the Pauline message, that *before God* there will be no difference between male and female. All discrimination of women will be overcome. And that will greatly contribute to the trustful acceptance of others in their otherness. Diversities will no longer be divisive, but complementary.

Adoration of the motherly tenderness of God, our Father

As soon as all dimensions and levels of the Church are marked by a joyous, regular Eucharistic celebration and by a corresponding theology, teaching and shepherding, all will learn to look more gratefully to the motherly tenderness of God, the Father of our Lord Jesus Christ. Women will be listened to as well as men. Thus the creation of man and woman in the likeness of God will be better understood and guide us to a better vision of God's motherly kindness, tenderness, compassion and mercy.

In the praise of his tender compassion and mercy the Church will be closer to the downtrodden, the poor, the marginal people. The sin of self-righteousness will be strongly unmasked. Moral and pastoral rigorism will be detested — surely, not to the detriment of genuine Christian morality.

There will no longer be any projection of human violence, human vindictiveness into the image of God.

The Church will fully honour Christ, the nonviolent Servant of God, the leader and model of therapeutic and liberating nonviolence. The Church will no longer bless armies and arsenals of mass-destructive weapons; she will no longer give any kind of justification to any kind of mutual threat of destruction. Fully committed to the conciliar process for peace, liberating justice and responsible conversion of the creation entrusted to humankind, the whole of Christianity will come to a deeper knowledge of the mystery of redemption for this world and the world to come.

All this will happen more easily if women participate as well as men in all decision-making processes in the Churches as

173

well as in wholesome societies. Women will also have their role in the Eucharist. In this climate, in which the mystery of redemption is seen in the light of Eucharistic faith-experience, sexual morality will be understood better, without any undue rigorism and thoroughly freed from the consequences of paternalistic, collective neurosis. In this field, too, inculturation will no longer be looked upon with suspicious anguish, but with trust in the Holy Spirit who works particularly in and through the Eucharist communities and their faith-sharing as well as sharing of life-experience.

By right understanding of the doctrine on the Eucharistic sacrifice, liberated from empty ritualism and from any kind of projection of vindictive justice and male-power into the image of God, the faithful will be better and more deeply motivated to renounce everything which contradicts the adoration of the motherly tenderness of God and religious respect for the dignity of each human person.

The Eucharistic people will, in shared effort, overcome all kinds of resentment, vindictiveness and violence. They will learn the central commandments of mercy, compassion, nonviolence: 'Be merciful even as your Father is merciful' (Lk 6 : 36). The Eucharistic people and communities will learn this not by abstract norms, but by always looking at the Holy Redeemer, the nonviolent Lamb of God, the compassionate healer. Thus learning from Jesus, the nonviolent and therapeutic compassion and love of enemies will make Christians pioneer peacemakers everywhere and on all levels. All this will never be severed from the adoration of the motherly tenderness of God in Jesus Christ.

The biblical virtues in the light of Eucharistic faith-experience

Moral teaching based on the decalogue and the Stoic cardinal virtues had little to do with Eucharistic faith-experience and with the history of salvation.

When the Eucharistic fundamental right is restored to all the faithful in all cultures, and when no discrimination of any kind is tolerated then all will find a new access to the basic biblical (eschatological) virtues.

We shall open ourselves to all the wonders God has done in the past by a Eucharistic 'grateful memory'. It will engrave itself in all our thinking and especially in all our motivations.

Eucharistic faith-experience lives, by the presence and ever new coming of Christ our Saviour, the basic virtues of the present moment: vigilance, watchfulness, readiness and discernment. Thus believers will better honour the signs of the times. Their individual consciences and their consciousness of solidarity will be more creative in discernment and readiness, more strongly motivated to honour the present moment in the Lord's saving presence. The Eucharistic faith-experience is open to all the dimensions of history: by gratitude (grateful memory to the past), by a vigilant discernment of the grace of the present moment, and not least to the *future* in all its wealth for this world and the world to come. The Eucharistic Church communities are the pilgrim people of God, open to every new challenge of history, ready for the necessary changes and adaptations to new opportunities and new needs. The promises for everlasting life in God's kingdom will also motivate hope-filled responsibility towards future generations. This vision of the Eucharistic memorial will certainly bear fruit in gracious sharing of all the natural and religious gifts, of the charisms and of the wealth of earthly goods.

Thus the otherwise good social doctrine of the Church will no longer hang in the air, but be rooted and perfected through the Eucharistic faith-experience and the sharing in the body and blood of our common Redeemer.

In the same vein I foresee an ever new discovery of the beatitudes and the goal commandments (Mt 5). Christian morality will no longer be falsified and sterilized by a rather static viewpoint and by overemphasis on the prohibitive norms.

I have no doubt that in this Eucharistic vision and motivation, well grounded prohibitive norms will be better, easier and more meaningfully observed, integrated in a liberating, hope-inspiring dynamics.

Thus the Church as teacher under the only Master, Jesus Christ, will be found more faithful to the basic truth and good news: 'You are no longer under law, but under the grace of God' (Rom 6 : 14). The Church will, by her whole conduct and renewed structures testify with the Apostle of the Gentiles:

'My present bodily life is lived by faith in the Son of God, who loved me and gave himself up for me. I will not nullify the grace of God; if righteousness comes by law, then Christ died for nothing' (Gal 2 : 20-21). Serving God with gladness we can rejoice living life in Christ Jesus. The Church of the twenty-first century will ever better understand St Paul's words: 'What Christ has done is to set us free' (Gal 5 : 1).

Moral pedagogy as paraclesis

The goal of the pedagogy of Church is the full stature of maturity of the faithful by a life guided by the Spirit and a deep knowledge of Christ. Only if Church authorities trust the faithful to grow up as Eucharistic persons, living creatively, guided by a sincere and well-informed conscience, 'under the law of grace', clearly oriented by the beatitudes and goal commandments, shaped by the biblical virtues of gratitude, vigilance-readiness, discernment and hope-filled respons- ibility, can she make the greatest gift to society and culture: the responsible citizen.

Therefore in the coming Eucharistic age, as I like to foresee it, Church authorities will not see their main business as in- culcating numerous exceptionless prohibitive norms (some of them poorly worded and less than convincing). Under the guidance of the only Master and Teacher she will use all the available competence and wisdom to help all to grow up for clear discernment. Thereby the main emphasis will not be on warning against fault, but rather encouragement in the power of the Holy Spirit. We call it *paraclesis*: this biblical word, frequently used in the Pauline letters, draws our attention to the Paraclete, the comforter, enabler and advocate who will call to mind what Jesus has taught us by his example and word (Jn 14 : 16.26; 15 : 26; 16 : 7). We shall never lose heart, because we are assured of the *'paracletos'*: 'to plead our cause to the Father' (1 Jn 2 : 1). The letter to the Philippians best describes the charism of *paraclesis*: 'If then our common life in Christ yields anything to stir up the heart, any loving consolation, any sharing of the Spirit, any warmth of affection or com- passion, fill up my cup of happiness . . with the same love for one another . . . and a common care for unity' (2 : 1).

In the renewed Eucharistic liturgy, following the tradition of the Eastern Churches the *'epiclesis'*, calling upon the Eucharistic gifts the power of the Spirit to make them the body and blood of Christ for us, and on the participants that by the same loving power of the Spirit they may become an agreeable gift to the Father is the springboard to the understanding of *paraclesis*. We believe truly in the Eucharistic presence of the Risen Lord turning our mind and heart to the saving truth that on the cross Jesus was not only out there, but absolute presence to the Father and to all humankind by offering himself in the power of the Spirit. Through the epiclesis and *paraclesis*, the Holy Spirit enables us to accept this self-giving presence of Jesus and to entrust ourselves unreservedly to him and to the Father, in the service of humankind.

By a Christological and pneumatological moral theology and moral pedadogy we are helped to understand Christian life as freedom in Christ in order to be 'led by the Spirit' (Gal 5 : 16-18) and to bring forth the 'harvest of the Spirit: love, joy, peace, nonviolence, kindness, goodness, fidelity, gentleness and self-control' (Gal 5 : 22).

Let us concentrate our endeavours, petitions and hopes on the building up of truly Eucharistic communities of human size and a Trinitarian spirituality which is at the heart of the Eucharist. Then the Church will overcome the frosty moralistic crisis and neurosis, and will be able to create everywhere a climate of mutual trust and encouragement. This will be the fulfilment of the hopes created by the Second Vatican Council. Then also the role of the successor of Peter will become more attractive as of one 'presiding' the world-wide celebration of redeemed and redeeming love, a servant and witness to the faith in the *Paracletos*, the comforter, the enabler, the advocate of trust and unity.

I would like to foretell that in the twenty-first century the article of faith, 'We believe in the Holy Spirit, the giver of life' will find a deeper understanding in the context of renewed Eucharistic communities, in all parts of Christianity.